Spirit Motivator

By

Dominic Zenden

Strategic Book Publishing
New York, New York

Strategic Book Publishing
An imprint of AEG Publishing Group
845 Third Avenue, 6th Floor - 6016
New York, NY 10022
www.StrategicBookPublishing.com

ISBN: 978-1-60693-998-7
SKU: 1-60693-998-X

Printed in the United States of America

Dedication

This book is for Katie.

Acknowledgements

This book could not haven been written without the ongoing support and friendship of Pat Senior, her husband Charles who also should not be forgotten. Thank you for making this possible.

My very dear friend Gail. You have made life easy and hard by being the person you are. Making me look at situations without mercy.

Neil Fellowes for allowing me to use his own personal research on Electronic Voices. Amazing proof of life after life.

I also wish to thank all the other people who have enhanced my knowledge and illuminated my understanding of spirit. Hazel and Victor stand out like a beacon of truth. Both now in spirit, still guiding and supporting, I have much to thank you both for. My growth as a medium and a man is in part down to your wonderful friendship.

I feel very humble to have met so many lovely people in my life; this book is only possible because of those people.

Thank you one and all.

Table of Contents

Chapter One

Love and Guidance

I lay transfixed in my wooden-framed bed, blankets stretched over my head, scared to move. It was two o'clock in the morning the house was quiet. Everyone else was upstairs, I was by myself downstairs, not even daring to breathe. I could hear somebody walking outside my window, the footsteps got louder; my heart was about to burst. Then, without warning, I felt a calm, soft, gentle voice envelope my world of fear. I lay still. I felt the words like a golden wave. Although I didn't realize it at the time, it was my first contact with spirit. I was six years old. The voice belonged to my grandfather George, a man who I had only met once, a fleeting encounter with an old man with gray hair and a deep throaty cough laying on his deathbed, extremely ill with bronchitis. He was warm and friendly with an ever-ready smile. So that night when he came close, it felt so natural. I never thought of him as a dead person, just Granddad.

I must have fallen back to sleep because the next thing I heard was the voice of my mother, very much alive. Her friendly but harsh voice was telling me, "Come on now, time to get up, you can't go to school with no breakfast." With the innocence of a child looking for his mother's approval, I found

7

myself telling my mum that Granddad George had spoken to me the previous night. I didn't get the response I was looking for. Her face turned into a frown. "Don't talk silly, when you're dead you're dead, enough," and with a small peck on the cheek she sent me on my way to school. My head was full of conflicting opinions, the last thing I was thinking about was school.

Mrs. Kird, in her schoolmistress tone, was what was waiting for me. I hated the smell of the old wooden classroom, the stench of bleach, humiliation of getting things wrong. I'm sure I didn't see the world like everyone else did. I would sit and daydream, watching the clouds of color coming from the sounds of everyday happenings. The school bell would ring out in a red and dark green cloud, excited voices of my class mates would appear yellow blue and orange and Mrs. Kird's voice was dark red with annoyance. At that young age I thought everyone saw the colors. It never crossed my mind that they wouldn't. But I knew I was different. What I didn't know at the time was that I was looking at the energy field that surrounds every single object, "the aura," the sensation of sound. There, in front of my eyes, vibrating sounds turned into wishy-washy colors. Even my friends didn't see things like I did.

As a small child I had no fear. No fear of water or of heights. I loved to swing on the biggest frames pushing myself to the very top of the bar, then jump off landing in a heap on the tall lush green grass. I would climb the tallest trees, often way beyond the limits of safety. I just had no fear. I also understood that you could never die. I've always known that the spirit world is next to our world, just an arms length away, a different dimension, a higher vibration of sound and vision; two other experiences had confirmed that to me.

My granddad George would pop into my thoughts from time to time his warm rich voice a friend among friends. But he would never push; if I didn't want him in my mind he would leave me in peace, I learned that thought was a powerful way to communicate how I was feeling especially with the spirit that I was sensing more and more. Friends wanting to talk, I wanted to climb trees kick footballs at brick walls build dens and do the things that a seven-year-old boy wanted to do. This was about to change. In the course of two weeks I saw two children killed by horrific accidents.

The first was a girl called Katie; she was seven, the same age as me, full of life and devilment. We caught the same school bus; one shilling (five pennies) each way for the three-mile trip. But you could save two pennies by getting off the bus on the return journey a mile from the houses and walk along the footpath. Many of us used to do that. We spent our two pennies in the sweet shop, crossed the road and then walked home. I still remember that September day, when we got off the school bus early to buy our sweets. It was a still autumn afternoon.

We would break up into little groups of friends laughing and shouting swapping sweets. All I can remember was crossing the road with my two friends. Katie was on her own and about a minute behind us; girls would always take a lot longer choosing. We heard the screech of brakes and the sickening thud. It was so fast and Katie was dead--killed in an instant. She didn't see the lorry that killed her. Although in shock, my instincts told me she had just passed over into spirit. I knew she was safe. Katie had opened the door to another world. I could sense her laughter echoing around my consciousness, a bird being released from a cage. I had never experienced a unique sensation like this. Total joy filled my heart; the whole sky spun, people were running round like toy soldiers and all I wanted to do was punch the air in celebration of a soul finding its way back home.

The second girl who died was only three; I didn't know her though I knew her brother. She was riding her tricycle outside her house just a street down from where we lived when a lorry reversed over her. She had no chance. Again I knew she was safe, set free from her human existence, even though I felt the pain of her mother. She was so caught up in her grief that she couldn't sense her little girl tugging at her dress.

I could. I wanted to shout out "Your daughter is with you. Look she wants to hold your hand." I so wanted to tell her but my mother, who already had me booked into the doctor for "tests" because she was worried about me, wouldn't have liked it much. Looking back now I realize that I had to go through these experiences to fully understand and believe in spirit. The knowledge that life is eternal is a gift to be given. It allows you to look at life totally aware that the body is just the vessel that holds the soul.

What is it about life? Just when you think you have it all sorted out in your head something happens and throws a spanner in the works!

I was a happy eight-year-old boy with normal friends, likes, and dislikes. I knew that when you died you didn't die. It was very straightforward to me in my simple world. Everywhere I looked colors flew back at me. If a dog barked I saw sheets of violet and blacks. I would watch airplanes fly over my head with dark browns and blues rapped around the engines like Christmas presents; it was normal to me. Yet here I was sitting in a gray walled waiting room because my mum said, "I wasn't normal!"

Of course I was normal; I liked football, jelly, sickie sweets, even girls; nothing seemed wrong. Yes, granddad George would come and spend time talking about me. He was always interested in how my football skills were improving and whether or not I had made any new friends. This was my secret. I could never share my insights. I kind of liked it that way; I didn't have to explain something that grown ups either didn't want to understand, or couldn't. So here I was sitting in the doctor's waiting room at the age of eight. My parents thought I was schizophrenic just because I could talk with dead people, see wonderful colors and had no fear of death. In my mind, I was the sane one.

The door opened and I was ushered into a light room with pictures of animals on the walls. A small rather boffin-looking man sat at the other end of the room looking at me over the top of his glasses. "Please sit down"; his glance guided me to a chair which was placed at a desk. A pen and pencil, a series of white question papers, some wooden blocks, a cage with a tiger inside, and a few other objects I fail to remember were laid out on the table. "So young man, you see colors around objects do you?" His voice was friendly and inquisitive. I nodded. He continued, "And you hear your grandfather George talk to you?" Again I nodded. Why would you ask me such questions I thought? Pointing to himself, "Young man what colors do you see around me?"

Nervously I spoke, "Blue in your voice, but the colors around your shoulders are very dark," I found myself saying. Now I had his attention. I could see he was intrigued.

He took a small flashlight from his top pocket and came closer. "I want you to follow the light for me please; from left to right, now look down to your left, and up to your right." "Very good" he said to himself as he marked the chart on his desk. These tests went on for what seemed liked hours. In fact there were ninety minutes of questions, filling out test papers, medical checks of eyes ears and chest. No stone was left unturned. When the results came back two weeks later I was pronounced normal with a very good imagination and a high IQ for my age. This was good enough for my mother. She accepted that her son was the same as everyone else's; just a little boy wanting to have fun. But what she never knew was that from that day onwards I talked to my grandfather George with increasing frequency. I just never told a soul.

My childhood was a steep learning curve. I spent hours in second-hand bookshops looking for books about life on other planets. From a young age I believed that for every star in the sky there was a planet with intelligent life.

My views today, some thirty-five years later, haven't changed. In fact they have grown stronger with knowledge. As a ten-year-old boy I was the only one in class who read about UFO's. I loved to read books about close encounters with Aliens. Betty and Barny Hill were the first people I read about who were abducted and taken aboard a spacecraft. I devoured every page, reading the details over and over.

11

My father, a rather cynical man with a bright intelligence and ready temper, was never a man to argue with. "When you're dead you're dead" he would say without giving it a second thought. He would continue, "Bloody aliens. Why would they ever want to come this god-forsaken planet?" while looking at my latest ten pence book I bought from the second hand bookshop. I wouldn't say anything. No point, he was right--he always was.

However, there was more than one way to get even. My dad used to smoke; never saw him without a cigarette in his hand and his morning routine was predictable.

At 7:00 a.m. he got up and went to the bathroom. Then I would hear him walking down the stairs, the sounds of rather loud farts . . . THURRRRRRRRRRR would follow him down the stairs. I would hear the sitting room door open with a squeak then Dad would sit down on his chair beside the table, reach for his cigarettes half asleep barely placing one between his lips, then click, click as the lighter lit the end. This would be followed by a loud chesty cough that filled the house.

I thought it would be funny to place a small firecracker in the end of his cigarette so when it was lit the end would explode with a loud bang!

I waited until everyone was in bed, crept into the sitting room, found his fags with his lighter on top ready for the morning. I reached out, opened the flip lid, took out the next two cigarettes and carefully pushed two firecrackers in each. Making sure everything was left just as I had found them.

Now all I had to do was wait. It was not easy under the circumstances. That was the longest night of my young life. Then I heard the familiar sounds of the toilet flush, of my father walking down the stairs with the normal accompaniment and the door squeaking open. I could almost see him reaching for his cigarettes fumbling to get one into his mouth. Please choose the right one I thought to myself. Then the moment of truth... Click... Click... slight pause then BANG! I waited for the shout as I imagined the ragged end of the cigarette hanging from his mouth. Tears rolled down my face, I could hardly control my laughter and sense of satisfaction of getting one over on him. My poor dad was very white that morning as he headed out for work unaware that he still had another cigarette just primed waiting to explode! I never owned up as I knew what he would do. It was my secret.

The house we lived in was nothing special; mid terrace with a dark blue front door the number ninety stood out in gold just above the letterbox. Out in front was a large wood; a place of paradise if you happened to be a ten-year-old boy who liked to climb trees. Out the back a medium sized garden with an apple tree, over the fence was a large playground with swings and round-a -bout, seesaw and two huge slides all surrounded by giant oak trees. I loved it. All my friends loved it too, I never wanted to be anywhere else in the whole world. But what I thought or wanted counted for nothing.

I have always been intuitive and at times, I hated being able to sense things. For instance; you know what someone is thinking before they open their mouth. This was one of these occasions.

My mum started with a bright enthusiastic voice, "We have some news for you." Yeah right I thought, this isn't news for me. She continued, "Your father has taken another job in Cambridge. That means we're leaving this house and moving in the summer holidays."

My heart sank. I just knew it, "That's only six weeks away." I heard myself say in a resigned voice that resembled our poor pet hamster that was buried in the garden the week before. Mum thought it was dead. I suspected it was just hibernating; it must have been one hell of a shock when he woke up three feet under!

I didn't want to say goodbye and to one special person I didn't have too. Katie would pop into my head often with her playful laughter and impish face. Over the next few months I relied on her to keep me smiling. It was so sad, leaving all my other friends behind. My whole world turned inside out; it seemed Cambridge was in a different universe. At least it might as well be. This was the lowest point of my life. I heard

13

my granddad George deep inside my head saying the same words over and over; like a ball thumbing against a brick wall. "It'll be all right; it'll be all right." All I could think of was new beginnings. Would my school be like the last one with smelly wooden classrooms and the smell of bleach?

I couldn't remember how long we had been driving. My head was in far away land, but when we turned the corner I came to with a jerk as the car slowed down to stop. "We're here," I heard my mum's voice from the passenger's side of the car. I looked out of the side window. There, in front of me, was our new home. A large blue and green moving lorry was parked at an angle on the driveway, men ran up and down the gang plank unloading big wooden boxes. I was impressed. The house was far bigger than my imagination lead me to believe.

I heard George say, "Told you, you would be alright" I had to agree.

I loved our new home. We had two toilets a large garden and I could see my new school from my bedroom. It was close enough to walk; no more catching the diesel-smelling clapped-out old red double-decker to school. It also meant I would have more time to make friends and get to know the local area.

In my last school I had lots of friends including Katie. This school was different. To start with it was a lot smaller, just over one hundred children ranging from five to twelve years old. I was close to my eleventh birthday so I joined the twenty-five older children who had been together since nursery school. Bad move. I went from loving school to hating it within ten weeks.

This experience taught me several lessons that I would be grateful for later in my life as a medium. One was to stand on my own two feet. I didn't need anyone to approve of who I was. Two was that being alone isn't such a bad thing. I had Katie who was kind and funny as I learned to listen to the voices in my head.

I look back at those days years later knowing that it was preparing me to face hostile or skeptical individuals who wouldn't accept the truth of life; the truth being that you never die. From that time onwards I knew I was special with a special gift that I had to share with others, Katie wouldn't have had it any other way.

As a teenager I never had an easy relationship with either of my parents. My mum was never in the same mood for two days in a row; she was kind and caring one moment, then impossible the next. I remember getting home from school and asking her innocently, "What's for tea Mum?"

"What do you want"" came the answer.

"Fish fingers please," then, without a warning, something happened that will stay with me for the rest of my life.

She shouted, "You Never Want Anything That I Have Got For You, You Ungrateful Child!" I couldn't believe what I heard. She had a way of making me feel guilty even when I hadn't done anything wrong.

I was no angel but I was never really naughty. I was too wrapped up in my world of spirit people, aliens, and football. I loved football, but neither of my parents were interested. I spent hours listening to my little blue potable radio; the commentator's voices brought the game alive in my head. I could smell the turf and fresh air as the noise of the crowd swayed from one side to the other. It was my escape. I would feel my grandfather George, who loved football too, sitting with me. I liked that because he made me feel safe.

My father wanted me to do well at school. I had little interest in math, English, and science, which frustrated him greatly. But I excelled at all sports, football, hockey, rugby, running, cricket, and basketball. I was on the school teams in all these sports. I was captain of the hockey and football teams, played county hockey and football as well as running for the county's cross country team with great success. These achievements went unnoticed. I felt I was born to the wrong parents. In those days I was like any normal teenager; I hated my parents.

My father wasn't a well man. Just after we moved into our new home he stumbled while walking down the stairs and fell to the bottom. He thought nothing more of it until he noticed his arms and legs felt stiff in the morning. He put it down to his age; he was forty-one. I would watch him try to lift his arms as he struggled to put his jumper on. The final straw was on bonfire night. While walking into the living room he slipped and put his legs through the bottom half of the window. It made one all-mighty bang which is why I remember the date. He was lucky to get way with a few cuts and grazes. But it made him realize that he had to go see his doctor; a very rare event in my dad's life. I don't remember him ever going to a doctor or dentist before then so I knew he was worried. His doctor, in a state of shock at seeing him, sent him straight to the hospital for tests.

When the results came back we were all in shock. He had Multiple Sclerosis, (This is a disabling neurological disease of the central nervous system. Eighty-five thousand young adults suffer from it in this country alone.) He knew he was going to die a slow horrific death. In the space of nine years, we watched him go from fit and healthy to a man who could not feed himself. The effects on family life were tremendous. For one thing his temper got worse; his illness overwhelmed both my parents. My mother couldn't cope with the situation and never hid the fact. My father was a trapped in his own personal hell with no way out except death. He was like a fly caught in a spider's web waiting to be eaten. This wasn't much to hold out for.

My dad didn't believe in God or life after death. He would say, "When you're dead your dead." He had had little time for me or my views. Over the next years I watched him die, a bitter and stubborn man, angry at being trapped in a body that was failing. It was the hardest thing I have ever been put through. I loved my dad for all of his faults but I didn't like him much. I was a self-centered teenager; hard to get through to unless you were speaking from spirit. I resented the fact that my father was ill. "Why couldn't he be like my friends dads?" I often thought; hence understanding between us was non-existent.

Our relationship went from bad to worse. I never listened to him or did anything he said. He would beat me but I got used to the pain. He would drag me from my room and throw me down the stairs kicking and punching. I would roll up into a ball until it was over, then crawl back to my bedroom crying. I went to school with black eyes and bruises on my legs and arms. I told my teachers that I was fighting with other children. After all he was my dad and I deserved it. He told me as much and he was always right.

My father died on December 21st at 6:00 p.m. I was with him when he died. In passing I could saw his soul lift out of his deformed body. I felt the same excitement that I had felt for Katie ten years earlier. I wanted to jump for joy; he was free.

That night something very special happened to me. I saw my dad as I remembered him before his illness. He had a soft gentle voice and was totally at ease with me. I felt a love that I had never felt from him; an unconditional sense of peace overwhelmed me.

He looked straight at me and I heard him say, "You were right son I was wrong; there is life after death." This was the first time ever he had admitted he was wrong about anything. From that moment to the present day I have a wonderful relationship with my father. He often comes to me to chat or just to sit and watch, discuss, understand, and laugh at me with my children.

My dad was in spirit for well over a year when my mum remarried a man I can only describe as weak. A whirlwind romance went from meeting to marriage in eight months.

My dad told me he was welcome to her. If he had lived he wouldn't have stayed; she was always a difficult person to live with. The only way to find peace was to let her have her way. Now she had found a man who always gave in to her demands while ignoring her mood swings. "A match made in heaven," my dad would say with a smile in his voice.

As for me, I moved out months ago. I wasn't welcome any more; mum's boyfriend gave me two weeks to leave. I only needed two days. I found a room with an elderly lady in the center of Cambridge. I have never forgiven my mother for what she did even though I know deep down she could never cope on her own. She was doing what she had always done;

anything to survive, even at the cost of losing her son. It was yet another lesson to learn.

I often think about those days and wonder if I could have changed anything. Was the direction I took the only way open to me? Had I decided on that direction before my life began or was I just born unlucky?

The obvious answer became clear in later life. I believe we choose our life path before we are born. We pick our parents, siblings, partners, and so on. This is the framework for learning our life lessons. We put ourselves in a position to create the circumstances that provide us with the situations we need for personal spiritual growth. Whether we take these opportunities or not is up to us. Free will coupled with synchronicity, "fate," meeting the right person at the right time. (I often think about 'what ifs?') How many people think of a past girlfriend or boyfriend; then wonder how different life would have been if they had chosen that person instead of their current partner? It's not far fetched to believe that our lives could be different if we made different decisions. To counteract this, I believe the choices we make before we are born are the crucial ones.

Before we are born we choose who our parents will be. They are the single biggest influence on our life from the start so we are create circumstances around us before we are born. To emphasize my point; how many choose life partners because they have similar characteristics to our parents? Or are total opposites? Either way we need to feel safe and secure so we make choices that are influenced by these needs.

I also think cell memory plays a big part in our current life choices. Let me explain:

For every lifetime we are born into our memory is wiped clean. But we retain knowledge of these lifetimes stored as a blueprint in every cell in our body. It's our personal record that stays with us through thousands of lives. We store all the accumulated knowledge; our likes, dislikes, good and bad deeds. Some may call it recorded karma. I think about it as cell memory. Every action we take has a reaction, every conversation has a consequence, and we are accountable to ourselves. We decide on the directions of our life and alternate the speed with which we evolve into spirit by the lessons we learn from the choices we make. This starts at the beginning with the choice of who our parents are going to be. I have learned that life is an ever-repeating circle. If we fail to make the right choices or take the wrong direction and fail to learn from situations, we come back and face the same situations until we resolve the issues. I think of this as our soul journey.

We have many lessons to learn and as many lifetimes as we need to learn these lessons. My guides, who I talk about later, point this out to me by stating that every soul has many thousand faces. I will talk more about my personal concepts, soul journeys, and soul partners later. For now it's enough to say life isn't just the here and now. It's the here and now after.

Time is a man-made way to order our lives while living the human experience. I will share with you something that happened to me when I was starting out on my spiritual path. This experience got me to think about time and whether or not it was a man-made concept to order our lives or a truly separate entity that is its own dimension.

As a young enthusiastic medium I was keen to learn and listen to older wiser mediums. I had so much to understand about everything. One man I call John, was a particularly close friend. We spent many hours chatting about paranormal worlds and debating the merits of the afterlife. John was always firm in his belief's; it was a matter of fact to him that the spirit-world was another dimension of our material world. I was young and needed proof before I could believe this, even though I had many contacts with so-called dead people. I had to experience what it was like for myself. So we agreed that whoever died first would make an effort to get back.

Time passed and I moved. I didn't see or speak to John much, only the occasional telephone conversation. It was always reassuring to hear his voice on the phone; we each talked about our progress. John was happy to give me the benefit of his vast knowledge gained over many years. I always looked forward to our telephone conversations; as infrequent as they became.

When the phone rang one warm summer evening in June, I was pleased hear John's reassuring and friendly voice. We talked about everything; people we knew, mediumship, even what it was like to die. It was our normal conversation and I thought nothing of it. The following September I found myself back in the town where John and I first met. Being a spontaneous person, I decided to visit the Spiritualist Church where I had met John all those years ago. It was good to see nothing had changed. It was like walking back in time; even the faces were the same. If this has happened to you, you have experienced the feeling of *déjà vu* that I did that evening.

I soon got to talking about past times, the mediums, the people who had come and gone, then the conversation turned to my friend John. I was happily related the last time I had spoken to him in June; he was in good form, full of life.

I was shocked when I saw a look of amazement on the faces around me, then sadness. "John died last May," one white faced lady told me. "Are you sure you spoke with him in June?"

I remembered the conversation. It was a hot early summer's day. I remembered telling him all about my platform performance the week before. Could it be that I had spoken to a man who died three weeks earlier? Did John keep his promise and come back to me to prove once and for all that life after death was a reality? Or did I go back in time with the memoirs and knowledge I already had? Either way the conversation with John raised many questions which remain unanswered twenty year later. Even now when the phone rings my heart jumps and I go back in time to that June evening.

It was early autumn; the leaves on trees were bright reds and golds. This is my favorite time of year. I love the smell of the early morning mist and crisp bite of the air. For the first time in my short life I had found happiness. I was always learning. I had a need to know about everything. I held endless conversations, in spirit, with my dad about what it was like to be dead, "No different," he would say with a tinkle in his eye but I knew it was. Thought is a very powerful thing in the spirit world. All you have to do is think of something and it was with you. I learned later that this is called "manifestation." At the time it didn't matter much. It was enough for me to know that if you thought about spirit it would be with you; not rocket science!

I could never work out why so many people make the spirit world out to be a monstrous place. I knew from a young age that we lived in one world separated by a thin veil.

My grandfather George and Katie had already given me all the evidence I would ever need to believe that the soul was eternal. My father was with me at a moment's thought, just a breath away. I felt like the bridge between these two existences. If I was to work along side spirit, like I felt I had to, I needed to know how the spirit world worked first. But was I seeking knowledge or wisdom? Every question was met by two others. My need to learn more was driving me insane. I didn't have to look too far for the guidance I so badly needed.

I woke up with a bump. It was early in the morning. I didn't want to be awake, "What do you want now?" I heard my inner voice shout. (I would get used to spirit people wanting to talk at inconvenient times--but in the early hours I ask you!)

This wasn't your usual spirit contact. As my eyes focused I saw a dark skinned man with large knotted plats of hair falling over his shoulders, large hook nose, and small kind dark eyes standing within breath distance over my head. He scared the life out of me! For a split second fear griped me. The memory of the footsteps outside my bedroom window flashed in front of me, then something I will always treasure happened. Without a word or seeing it I felt a strong hand touch my shoulder, then forehead. Be calm, be calm was in my thoughts with a feeling I can only describe as being hit by an electrical charge. I was transfixed not by fear but amazement. Then a shock wave of emotion hit me and tears streamed down both cheeks. Sobbing uncontrollably I knew this man. I had always known him. He was Red Cloud, not a guide but a mentor, teacher and friend. My life had moved on enough for him to show himself to me. I always knew that feeling of someone watching from afar, waiting for the right segment of my existence when I was ready to listen. This man was part of me in many past lives. Seeing him again was like returning home. I couldn't wait to start asking questions. But before that, there was only one question I could ask; "How can I help you?" This was the beginning of a life of service, not for spirit, but for me.

Chapter Two

Knowledge or Wisdom

I've never had a problem in believing in spirit. It's as much a part of my personal life as eating and breathing. From the moment I was born it didn't matter which way I turned, spirit found me. I was always going to work hand in hand with them. It is a privilege to be able to stand up on stage and give people messages from family and friends. I'm proud to be a medium, a mediator between the two stages of life, to share the knowledge that we never die, not by convincing people with my personal beliefs of the after life, but by bringing spirit through with clear and precise information.

Love is the only truth and love alone bridges the gap between the two worlds. That's why you should always send out thoughts of love to the people you would like to contact before you see a medium work or book a private sitting. That makes my job easier and you're far more likely to make contact. It's a win-win situation. My spirit guide Red Cloud, a spirit of few words, taught me to trust, not question. I found this very hard at the start. But as you train your mind to talk, the messages come through. I've had some very strange words to pass on over the course of time. I've laughed and cried, felt compassion and great happiness. But I always trust that spirit will come through with the correct way for me to give the right message to the right person. When I'm on stage looking across the sea of faces, I always know who the message is for because that person stands out; one recognizable face in an otherwise anonymous audience. After that person receives their confirmation, another face pops out of the crowd. This is because I trust spirit.

Red Cloud will come into my head saying, "Less is more." Remember everyone has come for his or her own message. You have a duty to reach as many souls as you can. I always remember the lessons of the early days. Spirit has a way of teaching you like no other.

One of my first private sittings was for a young lady. I can see her face today as clearly as if she is standing beside me. Her bright blue eyes, clear rosy complexion, blond shoulder-length hair added to a warm, ear-to-ear smile. I relaxed the instant I opened the door. That isn't always the case, especially when I first started doing sittings. She followed my glance as I ushered her in to my little room. It was nothing fancy, just a wooden table covered in a lace cloth, two high back Victorian chairs with bright red padded seats, a few crystals placed to the side, a jug of water with two glasses and my scent burner filled with my favorite Eucalyptus oil. I pulled the chair out for her. She smiled and sat down.

What happened next was to stay with me always. As I started to open up all I could focus on was The Star Trek Ship Enterprise. I had a vision of The Enterprise right in the middle of mind where spirit would normally appear.

I heard the soft voice of Red Cloud. All he said was "Trust."

So I cleared my voice and began "You're not going to believe this but all I can sense is the Star Trek Ship Enterprise!"

With this the lady went white, tears rolled down her cheeks, she jumped out of her chair, flung both arms around my startled neck, mascara ran down her face like two huge spiders: all I heard was, "Thank you, thank you so much." I've had reactions but never like this. I could hardly believe what I was witnessing.

Still trembling, the lady returned to her chair but now that lovely smile had returned. Her face lit up from the mouth upwards. I could tell she was at ease, like a person who had found the answer to a crossword puzzle that was driving them mad. She started to talk, "My dad died four years ago." I listen intently. "Before he died we decided on a phase that he would use if he could ever get back through to us. The phrase was The Star Ship Enterprise; something no medium could guess. I've been listening for that phrase ever since!"

Now tears were streaming down my face. I felt a warm sense of emotional release.

"Thank you. You have said something I had lost hope in ever hearing."

I was so pleased I had trusted, I could have easily dismissed this and moved on. Before she left she handed me a small box "I would like you to have this. It belonged to my father. I always said that the person who gave me proof beyond doubt that my father had survived was who I wanted to have it."

How could I refuse?

"Look after it for me won't you?" she said with a smile.

I had no idea what I expected so I nodded.

We embraced and that was that. She left the way she came; with a large bright smile on her face and with one major difference. Now she knew life was eternal and love would always find a way back.

I learned so much from that sitting. First was to trust whatever I was sent by spirit. Second was that less was more. One phrase was enough to prove survival; no need to go on and on.

If you ever want to arrange to make contact with a loved one, take time to agree on a phrase or a few words that mean something to you both while you're together. Even after a separation for whatever reason, you can send your thoughts out to that person in spirit with the phase or words that would have meant something to you both.

Spirit comes so close that all you can hold your hand at arms length to see how close. I feel the frustration from spirit who senses the thought and love coming to them but can't quite knock that door down. We often feel too sorry for ourselves to sense them. You never know; this simple belief might just make the difference between knowing beyond doubt that the medium you are with has a link to your loved one.

Oh yes: I'm sure you want to know what was inside the box don't you? It was a Rolex watch worth over £2000. I keep it as a reminder of that day. It's also a reminder that you can have all the money in the world but it means nothing without love. Listen and learn from everybody you meet because as a medium it's my everlasting goal for perfection.

When people ask me, "How do I become a medium?" "How do I contact my spirit guides?" these are two simple questions that I'm not sure I have the right to answer. I've always known that spirit was there. But I also know that I've had to work extra hard to convince myself that I should do this work. It's not a choice, but more a way of life. Mediums are born not made.

Having said that; I believe that we all have the ability to connect to spirit. Like anything in life, the harder we work the better we become. Ask yourself if you are willing to restrict your life? Are you willing to restrict the food you eat, the exercise you take, personal time management and make everything right so you can put out maximum effort?

My first tip for budding mediums is; think very carefully before you set foot on your journey of service to spirit. If you feel you can do all the above then, seek out knowledge. I'm willing to spend time with people, talking and explaining. The way I look at it is the more people who work with spirit the easier my life becomes! Mediums should work together, helping, caring, and looking out for one another. It's not about making money or personal ego; without spirit we are nothing. It's about trusting what you know deep down.

So what do we know deep down? Where does our thinking originate? Is it just from us? Or do we have thoughts placed among the thoughts we think?

This is what I believe. Thought is very powerful; we are what we think we are. Our thoughts can reach out into the universe and beyond and influence others in ways we can only imagine. In order to understand and control our thinking we must become more aware of what starts the thought process. In everyday life we work on autopilot. We wake up, get dressed, and eat, all things we do daily without thinking about it. We don't give a second thought to breathing, but as soon as we think about the rhythm we become aware of so much. We pay attention to how our heart beats, how we feel inside; this is what thought does for us. We become aware of the world around us. Once we learn to separate our own thinking from that of our guides' it can make us more aware of the spirit world. Only then can we see how much more we can feel. Once you become aware of your guide's thoughts it's like finding a heartbeat. We learn to listen and trust which allows us to work alongside spirit. It's the first step in understanding.

So how can we separate out our thoughts? First, you must recognize what mood you are in and what makes you happy? Or what makes you sad, angry, tried, hungry? Learn about your thinking. Learn about things you do without thought. It isn't that hard. We do it every day without thinking why. If we stop and think why, we will recognize our trigger thoughts. When you know how you think, it's easier to find the thoughts that don't fit into your own pattern. These are your guides' thoughts. When you start to listen you will find yourself picking up books you would normally walk past and ask questions you would never have considered.

I have found over the years that music helps me sort out my thinking. Here is what I do: I listen to music and separate out the different instruments by listening to just one part of the tune at a time. I focus on the voice, then the drums and so on. Do this and you might find a piece of music or a song you have listened to all you life sounds much different. We miss a lot by not thinking about it.

Spirit helps us in many ways even if we don't want them too. A friend whose brother died the year before phoned me. She couldn't find the iron cross he had left her. She wore it constantly, only taking it off and placing it next to her bed at night. This morning she woke up, started to put on the cross and found that it wasn't where she left it. The cross was the only thing she had from her brother so when I answered the phone her voice was low and she was very upset. "You must try and help me. I can't find it anywhere," she sobbed.

But this wasn't about finding her cross. This was about making me aware that she hadn't been taking her medication. Her brother was worried about her. He came through in an instant. "It's in the bathroom cabinet," I heard him say adding, "right next to her medication which she has failed to take for the last week."

I thanked him for the information and reassured him that I would talk to his sister. With that he was gone. "Have you been taking your medication? " I asked. That wasn't what my friend expected.

"No I haven't, not for about a week now!"

"Well your brother was worried about you. He got you to phone me by placing his iron cross right next to your medicine in the bathroom. He knew I would be the first person you turned to. He also knew I would pass the message on word-for-word. I continued, "If you had taken your medication you would have found your cross. Go look for yourself."

The phone went quiet while I waited. What seemed like hours was only seconds.

"Got it!" I heard her scream with delight! Right in front of her eyes was the iron cross in the cabinet right alongside the tablets she should have been taking. She was excited not only because she had found her iron cross, but by knowing her dear brother was still watching over and caring for her. I knew the message got through and I had played my part. Needless to say I never had to help her find that cross again.

Another time spirit helped a loved one for a totally different reason. By now word that I could help people find lost objects had got round. It wasn't me who found them; it was relatives and friends in spirit who were only too happy to be asked to help. All I needed was a link and the results were remarkable. This lady was also in a state. Most people contact a medium as a last resort after spending months looking for the lost item. I sat her down knowing she was a person who would not believe in spirit easily. "It's like this," she said, "my father died over six months ago and the family is in turmoil. We have looked everywhere but can't find his will. We know he made one because he remarried two years before he died. We thought his new wife was after his money, so he made a point of showing his will to us. I'm at my wits end. So I thought I had nothing to lose by coming to see you" That's nice I thought, she doesn't believe but she wants her money!

My thoughts soon turned to a spirit man. "I've been waiting for them to get in touch; it's the will isn't it?"

"Yes," I said inside my head.

"I want you to listen very carefully young man. Here is where they will find the will. In my new house is a small cupboard under the stairs. On the left hand side is a small shelf and at the back of the shelf is a wooden box. The box is empty but the lid isn't. It has a secret sliding panel. If you slid that panel in the lid they will find the will."

I passed this information on word-for-word along with other details like the man's name and how he died. The lady stared at me; I could tell she didn't believe me. The proof was in finding the will. She thanked me for my time and left. I thought nothing more of it. The next day there was a knock at the door.

Standing in front of me was this lady and two others. I had never met them but could tell they were sisters. "I had to see you," the lady said. "We've come to say 'Thank you'. I must admit that when you told me where to find the will yesterday I didn't believe you. But I went to my step-mums house all the same. I asked if I could look in the cupboard. I had to explain first, but the box was right where you said it was. I couldn't believe my eyes. I slid the lid open just as you described and there it was, the will."

She was grateful and amazed at the same time. But I knew she would find it. I never doubted what her father had told me. In this line of work little miracles happen every day.

The one thing I love about my work is the unpredictability; I never know who I might be talking to next or their purpose for walking through my door.

So when a lady in her sixty's booked an appointment one evening, I didn't give it a second thought. The lady was small, smartly dressed in a light gray trouser suit; her hair set in a gray mass reminded me of the pink candy floss I bought as a child. She looked tried and worried as she walked in and sat down. The lights threw dim shadows jumping on the ceiling from the light of my oil burner; the familiar scent of eucalyptus filled the air. Nighttime didn't matter as it was the end of the day for me. I had no other appointments booked and tomorrow was Saturday, my rest day. I felt no pressure to move fast. I relaxed letting spirit come close.

Bang! I was hit with the image of a lady looking up at me, her hair floating upwards, eyes large and starring unblinking, her naked body gray rotating backwards and forward. My mind reached out for recognition; this wasn't a person it was a dead body. Why would spirit show me a dead body? All I had ever seen before was images of people in spirit with voices telling me who they were. This was different. I was looking at the empty shell of a persons body under water, no sound, just pictures. What should I do? Should I come out and say what I was seeing? Or should I try to clear this picture and move on?

As a medium I was taught to trust and it was that trust that gave me the courage I needed to continue. Time stood still, the picture was overwhelming, the room disappeared, and I was standing on the shore of a large lake looking out at an old wooden jetty. The sky was deep blue, sun burning down on my neck, I felt myself talking, but I wasn't conscious of the lady sitting in front of me. I was able to describe everything I saw from the body buried deep in the water to the surrounding area.

It felt like seconds but it had been well over an hour before the picture faded away and the room came back into view. The scent of eucalyptus hit my nostrils, the light in my oil burner still flickering casting dancing shadows on the ceiling. The lady had hardly moved; listening intently to my voice not realizing that I was in the room. I smiled and began to apologize; she looked into my eyes, held her hand up to stop my words before they had even formed in my mouth.

It was her turn to talk and for me to listen. I can still hear the words for her story was a remarkable one.

She began. "What you have shown me tonight takes my breath away. I've been looking for my sister since 1965 when she vanished from the face of the earth. She lived in the United States with her husband. One minute she was there, the next gone. I've spent the last thirty years looking for her. What you have just shown me was one of the two lakes that she lived right next to." She continued, "I haven't dared to hope that she still might be alive. I believe if she were living somewhere else she would have been in contact. And she never missed a birthday."

I nodded: knowing what I had seen before describing the lake I knew her sister was dead. With a deep breath I told her what I had seen before I had started talking about the lake. I knew it was the right thing to do now. I couldn't think of this lady going another thirty years without knowing her sisters fate.

Her face dropped in a resigned reluctance. "Thank you." she whispered.

That evening stays in my mind. You never know what you might experience. There is a footnote to this story. She went back to the lake I had described but never found the body of her sister. Maybe it had been too long or maybe she had never been there at all. We might never know. But something I do know is that as mediums we may not always be able to find a happy ending or tie up lose ends. But the gift we have to help others find peace is beyond value. Ask the gray haired lady who walked into my room after thirty years of searching.

In this experience I talk about being taken away from my normal surroundings, being shown a place that I had no memory of. The lake was as real to me as if I was walking alongside its shores; but the fact was I sat in a room many miles away. How could that be? By now I realized that spirit was always teaching me something new but it was up to me to find the answers so I could understand the process. In my mind I thought that if I could master this skill it would be very helpful in finding lost people or animals or objects. It was about visualization. If I could sense the picture I could work to develop the skill of remote viewing.

Over the next few weeks I worked hard to learn this skill. It was to become my ability to picture through thought. I needed a voice link, a photograph or an item to hold (psychometrics) to feel the picture that would appear in my mind. But trusting what I was seeing was the hardest barrier to overcome.

The only way was to start working with it. If I got good results I would know for sure; but like most things, I had to wait for someone to contact me. I knew if spirit wanted me to work with visualization the phone would ring when I least expected it.

There are times in life that you could happily turn over and go back to sleep. This was one of those. It was early on a Saturday morning. I always panic inside when the phone rings at such times. Nobody would call unless it was urgent I told myself as I reached over the bed and picked up the receiver. "Hello," I said in a low go away voice.

"Are you that psychic that finds lost people the voice demanded," not even a hello back!

"Yes that's right, but do you know what the time is?"

He didn't answer my question. His voice was desperate, "I need you to find my girlfriend she been gone for over a week. She has no medication with her and I'm afraid she might die if she has an attack. She has very bad asthma and without her steroids there is a good chance she won't make it."

Now he had my attention. I was wide awake. I knew this was the test; I had to help him. So two hour later I was sitting in a freeway service area looking at a photograph and holding clothes that belonged to this girl. A freeway service area isn't the best place for peace and quiet. This was going to be a true test of not only my skills but my concentration. I had no need to worry.

The picture was very clear. I could see the road layout. I was looking down on the left at the top of the road. There was a large group of shops. I could feel myself being pulled down the road; on the right was a MacDonald's. I was being shown into the city center and although I didn't realize it at the time, the route I was taking was the route she would have walked from her home to the basement flat where we found her a few hours later. She was safe and sound and had stopped with a friend for no other reason than she needed some time to herself. She was unaware of the trouble she had caused.

I felt very proud that I could find somebody in a large city but I had one last surprise. I was mailed the front page of the local newspaper two days later was big bold print "PSYCHIC FINDS MISSING GIRL." With the simple note attached Thank you.

Not all searches are so dramatic. For every person who comes to me for help their need is always very urgent. I have heard lines like "You're my last hope." "If you don't find it I don't know what I will do." No pressure there! Some searches end in sadness. Old dogs who are faithful friends to their owners for years will go off to die by themselves leaving the owner heart broken and I have to pass on the sad news. I do try to warn owners about this before I start looking. Without exception people come back saying I would rather know the truth than live in hope. As long as I have a photograph or the dog's blanket I can normally sense if it's passed into spirit. If the dog is still alive I will get a snap shot of the area surrounding the dog at that time. If I match that with a local location, the dog isn't far away. I have reunited many owners with their pets by scent trailing. This is done by taking an article of clothing belonging to the owner and dragging it along the ground in a one to two mile radius around the home; then back to the door. Simple! I've known dogs to be sitting outside the house before the owner got back. All they needed was a map to follow. Humans search with our eyes but dogs, cats, and many small animals search with their noses.

Cats are challenging, independent creatures that come and go at will; loyalty doesn't even come into the equation. So when a cat goes missing it can be extremely difficult to trace. I've lost count of the many cases where I've found the cat a few doors away with its new owner saying they thought it was a stray! September is the worst month for missing cats. They go after field mice as the farmers bring in their crops and stay away for four or five weeks. They return to their grateful owners a little thinner but unaware of the fuss they have caused... I'm always happy when September has passed; it means my phone doesn't ring half as much.

Birds are almost impossible to find. Once they have flown away they are usually gone for good. On one occasion I found an African Blue Parrot who had flown from his owner's shoulder. She forgot the parrot was there when she went outside to put trash in the bin. The parrot couldn't believe his luck and flew up into the nearest tree before you could say "pieces of eight." They got him down three days later by bribery; a large red apple.

The last story I will tell you about is the most expensive item I found: A diamond earring worth £20,000! Spirit also had a hidden agenda.

A nice lady reporter phoned from the local newspaper. "Are you the psychic gentleman who finds lost objects?" she asked, not knowing if she had the right person. She went on, "I read about how you found that young girl and I hope you can help me." I had never turned anyone away and wasn't about to start with her.

I assured her I would do everything I could for her but I needed to know what she wanted me to look for.

"I don't want a story." she said, "This is for me. My boyfriend brought me an expensive pair of earrings; gold with diamonds set into the surface." I heard her take a deep breath, "They're worth over twenty thousand pounds. I have one but can't find the other."

I didn't even need to think. Into my mind came a picture of a black and white purse. "Do you have a black and white purse?" I asked.

"Yes," came the reply. "That's what I keep them in."

"Have you looked inside that purse?" Stupid question I thought, but I was sure that's where it was to be found.

She told me that not only had she looked inside but she had also turned the purse inside out with no luck.

"Look again I think you might just be in luck."

As happens on these occasions there was a brief silence then a scream. There in front of her in her purse was the other diamond earring, winking at her like it had been there all the time. Now that could be the end of the story but you know it isn't going to end there. Spirit works in funny ways. If they want you to do something, people are placed into your life. This lady wasn't just a reporter on a local newspaper, she was the editor! This was my link into writing; something I had never thought of before, though spirit had. That earring had disappeared for a reason.

We all need some peace and quiet at times. I'm no exception. I don't like crowds. If I go shopping it is early in the morning; far less noise. I seldom go watch football live unless I'm lucky enough to be invited into a VIP box which happens once in a while. Being able to feel people's thoughts can be very disturbing in large crowds or in small rooms. Knowing what someone is thinking isn't always nice. That's why I need my own special place inside to go when I want to be away from everything living.

If you have ever felt the same way let me explain how I escape.

I make sure I won't be disturbed. I light my oil burner with eucalyptus oil as the scent helps me. Smells can be good at taking you back. Thinking about cut grass or tarmac takes my thoughts back to the house near the woods where I played with my friend Katie. It works like magic. Something in my subconscious triggers thoughts. I associate eucalyptus scent with my visualization of spirit. I have my own old oak tree, a large hollow tree that stretches way up into the sky like a giant waking up. Inside the base is an old wood door which I open with a struggle. I peer inside and barely see a shaft of warm golden light coming from the very top of the tree. A damp stone staircase and the smell of wood fill my nostrils. I can taste the moist air and feel the cold stone under my feet as I start to climb; slowly at first then faster as the door below disappears into the gloom. I stop halfway to catch my breath, and then resume my climb up the remaining steps to the warm light at the top of the tree. At the top I push open the small trap door and scramble through it head first and land in a warm meadow filled with lush green grass, buttercups, and daisies. In the distance is a fresh young fruit tree which I walk to. I pick a piece of fresh ripe fruit, sit down, and eat. I feel the sweet warm juice run from my month and down my neck, the hot summer sun is warm and relaxing. I lay down and sleep. (This is my own private place. Everybody should have their own place where they can escape.) When I'm ready, I reverse the journey until I'm back in the room.

Try it yourself. It doesn't have to be a tree; it can be anywhere in the universe. Let your senses and imagination take you there. It might even change how you see time.

My interest in time has taken me on some long journeys. I have met people who claim to have traveled back in time and the one common link between them is the lack of understanding of what is happening.

One couple had a remarkable experience. This story is one of my favorites because they didn't realize what had happened until they tried to return to the quant little Devonshire village they had passed through while driving their car on holiday.

The couple were driving around the Devonshire countryside when they came across a road climbing up a rather steep hill. They were not able to turn around so the man pressed on. He had to put the car into low gear to barely creep up this steep, difficult hill. They felt relief when they reached the summit and saw a small town below them. In exhaustion from the climbing experience, they couldn't wait to get to the bottom of the hill and explore the small village. On driving into the village they noticed how old world it looked. It was like a film set designed to take viewers back some twenty years. People were busy in their daily lives, dressed in old-fashioned clothes. Cars looked to be in remarkable condition considering their age. Even the shop signs looked different. This was truly a quaint Devon village. The couple spent an hour or so looking round, enjoying the slow pace of life and easy going atmosphere before driving on. They made a metal note to return later with friends to show them this special place they had discovered. A few days later, with their intrigued friends, they set off to find the old world village. But try as they might they could not find a single clue to the whereabouts of this unique place.

What did they discover? Did they go back in time to a place that no longer exists? What they saw was real. I've no doubt as both stories were told identically and they had no reason to make up a tale. I personally believe that they went back in time without realizing it.

Another story that I learned of was told by a man who lived in New York City. He was standing on a corner waiting to cross the street when he felt as if he was being dragged backwards through warm water without getting wet. This happened in the blink of an eye. As the feeling subsided he found himself in 1920's New York. The landscape had changed, tall skyscrapers had disappeared, and traffic was now a mix of horses and cars. The disorientation was fleeting but its happening confirms that time slips are real. It also confirms that we never know when we might be whisked back to a distant age in the past.

This glimpse of the past only lasted a few moments; but it was a time slip. Fantastic, I hear you cry; time slips are real! How can I experience one of these events? The short answer is you can. You might have seen a ghost or experienced a feeling of *déjà vu*, but you would have had no control over when this happened. You were in the right place at the right time. These events happen at random.

Let me explain further. For centuries people have written about ghosts and strange occurrences; ghost ships at sea, people appearing then disappearing. These events happen when the right conditions occur in the environment. The energy of traumatic events is absorbed into the surrounding landscape or buildings waiting to be triggered by an electrical storm, a sensitive medium or some other force of nature that we are not aware of. Perhaps it is like turning on an invisible videotape that replays past events; hence we see things that might not fit in our current time.

I call this the Stone Tape Theory; an imprint of a past event being re-run before our eyes, a little piece of time just for us. However, this does not explain what happened to the couple in Devon. I think what happened to them was that they passed through a time fracture. They drove straight into a random event. In my understanding, time is a vast circle; no beginning, no end. It is where everything that has happened already exists and everything in the future already exists also. It is waiting for us to unravel it. In theory we can move either ahead or back while changing events by our personal actions.

So far we have only explored time shifts that go backwards. I have researched people who claim to have met their future self. This is the stuff of science fiction, but I have studied two cases that exhibit credibility. In the first; a man sat down in front of his TELEVISION one afternoon to watch the news. What was unusual about that was that he watched a terrible explosion happen at a power station in Wales. It was two o'clock on a Saturday afternoon as the reporter read the awful news with pictures of smoke bellowing into the sky and firemen running with hoses. People were being evacuated from nearby homes, covered in blankets with small children crying. The scene was chaos. With this, the man switched his TELEVISION to watch the Saturday afternoon sport. He made a mental note to catch the news later for an update. Around 6:00 p.m. that afternoon he switched his TELEVISION to see the latest power station news. There was nothing, not even a mention. He found this strange so he phoned his brother and asked him if he'd seen the news of the dreadful explosion in Wales. His brother had watched the news but didn't recall any news about a power station. Feeling perplexed he put the phone down and wondered if he had dreamt the whole thing. Imagine his surprise when the same report came on the news the next day; with the same footage he had seen one day earlier! He was on the phone to his brother right away. His brother confirmed the he was watching the same pictures. So what had happened? Did he watch the events unfold from Wales one day before the explosion took place? The only conclusion I can reach is that this man had moved forward in time for a few minutes.

The second story involves a lady in her mid twenty's. She is a normal person with nothing to gain from talking about her personal experience. In fact she was a little embarrassed by the whole thing but needed to understand what she had gone through even though the experience was to change her life. She was enjoying a quiet afternoon at home when there was a knock at the door. When she answered the door an elderly woman was standing in front of her. She looked familiar but she had never met this person before. Not wishing to be rude the younger lady asked how she could help. What happened next was remarkable. The older lady seemed to know much about her life and warned her that her life would be cut short if she carried on doing what she was doing. Feeling scared and angry the young woman shut the door and ran back into the house. Why would that old lady wish to upset her? How did she know so much about her life? Then something dawned on her. The woman at the door had the same diamond ring on her right hand that her Grandmother had given her two years earlier. Could it be pure coincidence? Or had she just met herself in forty years? We might never know, but the encounter made such an impression on the young lady that she changed many things in her life; it was a life-changing experience. Did she dream the whole thing? It's possible. I have known people to have dreams that predict the future showing the outcome of continuing along the same path. But this was different. I believe she really met her future self and was given an insight to the outcome of her life.

Dreams are a way of foreseeing the future. Do we go forward in time when we sleep? Dreams have been used to predict outcomes of wars and conflicts since we started fighting one another. Do psychics and mystics experience time slips, small visions of the future during sleep or meditation? Without doubt, it comes under claircognizance (clear knowledge), the universe knows everything! So in principal all we have to do is tap into that knowledge, I believe many can, some do.

Chapter Three

Past Lives

Being a medium opens up many questions. Far too many for me to start to list; but one area that I'm regularly asked about is Past Lives. This subject has fascinated me since I was a teenager. As an adult I was lucky enough to train as a Past Life regression therapist. This involves is taking people back into Past Lives to explore why something in this life holds fear for them; something they can't move past. Using hypnosis to unearth deep memories enables the person to see the reasons behind an irrational fear or the connection between certain places or people.

Here are some true stories about Past Life regression.

My office phone rang. Instinctively I reached out and lifted the receiver, "Hello. I don't want any of that tarot card nonsense," said a distinctive West Midlands accent!

"That's alright then," I said, "because I don't read tarot over the phone"

The lady's name was Gail. Something in her voice cried out for help. From the very first moment Gail spoke I didn't know whether or not I could help her. I sensed her plight was a difficult one but I knew we would be friends forever.

Gail was in a relationship with a man who was difficult to understand. He was an easy going charming, wonderful person. Gail had fallen for him the moment she set eyes on him. They moved in together, so very much in love. When Gail gave birth to a little boy their life was complete. Gail loved her child more than life its self but the relationship with the father was going down hill. He was still charming to everyone outside his family but failed to help with the child, often for days on end. He would accuse Gail of being unfaithful and check all her movements. For some reason he couldn't cope with being a father.

Gail and her son grew close. By the time they bought their first house together the relationship was failing, Gail was unhappy and felt trapped. The lack of trust was killing the relationship. They had massive fights and huge arguments. He threatened her saying if she ever left him for another man, he would kill her and their son. By the time I spoke with Gail, her life had reached a crisis point; she could no longer live the life he wanted her to live.

With great courage she threw him out. She was unable to cope with his paranoid behavior any longer. He went to live at his mothers. Gail was now alone with her son and was able to allow herself some breathing space. Her partner was still in the background, his dual personality still very much in evidence. Threatening phone calls were followed by calls stating his undivided love for her. During this time Gail's thoughts turned to another man. Although they were just friends, Gail was starting to fall for him. Without knowing it she was falling in love with another man who was kind, gentle and above all got on well with her son.

Then a bombshell dropped. This man, who was becoming more than just a friend in Gail's mind, decided to move overseas. Gail was devastated again. She was still getting mixed messages from her ex-partner. He had settled into a routine at his mothers but still wouldn't accept that Gail didn't want him. He did his best to persuade her that he was a changed man and how it would work if he moved back home with the two of them. After holding out for a long summer, she decided that she wanted to try again with her partner. He moved back home and they hoped for another child; Gail had always wanted a little girl. But things changed again. In late December, year her partner was taken ill, admitted to the hospital and died. Gail was inconsolable. She was alone with her life in pieces, all over again. Her partner was dead and the man she had fallen in love with was many thousands of miles away.

Six months later Gail was struggling to rebuild her life. Her weight had dropped alarmingly. It was at this stage that she asked me to regress her to see if we could find the answers to why she had taken this life road. Had her partner been with her before? Why did she fear losing her child? Why did she feel love for this man overseas?

What follows is a transcript of the session Gail went through, hoping to find those answers.

I started by taking Gail into the space between lives to see what she would recall.

"What do you see?"

"DARK"

"How do you feel?"

"SCARED THERE IS A LONG CORRIDOR IN FRONT OF ME. I SEE MIST, A BUILDING AT THE END WITH AN ARCHWAY."

"What do you see under the archway?"

"AN OLD MAN, HE HAS A BEARD, HE WANTS ME TO DECIDE."

"Decide?"

"DECIDE ON MY THOUGHTS."

"Are you still walking?"

"YES NOW I'M IN A COURTYARD. IT'S A CIRCLE WITH COBBLES ON THE GROUND AND A WELL IN THE CENTER. THERE ARE FIELDS WITH LONG GRASS."

"What are you wearing?"

"LONG DRESS, WHITE APRON, YELLOW SLEEVES."

"Are you still walking?"

"NO."

"What do you see?"

"A BIG TABLE "ROUND" IN TWO HALVES, ONE CHAIR BEHIND HIM, SEVEN MEN WITH DARK HAIR LONG ROBES, LOVELY LIGHT COMING FROM THEM, WANT TO SHOW ME SOMETHING."

"Show you what?"

"WHERE TO GO AT THIS POINT."

"Do you feel safe?"

"YES, SOMETHING TO DO WITH BEFORE, CALLED GERRARD. TALKING ABOUT THE YEAR WEIGHED DOWN BY THOUGHTS."

"MORE PEOPLE CLOSING IN. NOT AS IMPORTANT AS OTHERS."

"TALKING ABOUT 1912 BEFORE THE WAR. SOMETHING TO DO WITH ME. NO FACE'S LIGHT COMING BRILLIANT GOLD PROTECTED."

"SEVEN MEN IN WHITE ROBES HEAL YOU WITH ENERGY."

"GO ROUND THAT WAY, SEVEN MEN. ONE SAT IN THE MIDDLE OTHERS STANDING UP, THREE ON EACH SIDE."

"Tell me what you see? Do you feel warm or cold?"

"CAN'T TURN ROUND. OTHER THINGS WITH NO FACES, SHAPE NO FACE, NICE TEMPERATURE."

"DECISION TO MAKE."

"What year is it?"

"1810."

"How do you feel?"

"DON'T LIKE IT."

"Don't like what?"

"CRUEL TO ME."

"Who is?"

"MY HUSBAND HE HITS ME."

"How old are you?"

"TWENTY FIVE."

"How long have you been married?"

"ONE YEAR."

"Where do you live?"

"SMALL HOUSE."

"How many children do you have?"

"BABY GIRL, ONE LITTLE BOY. SCARED OF HUSBAND."

"MY FRIEND WILF WORKS IN THE FIELDS, GENTLE, CAN'T HAVE HIM; MY LITTLE GIRL IS WILF'S."

"What are you going to do?"

"TAKE CHILDREN AND GO. HUSBAND DOESN'T KNOW. SCARED HE MIGHT FIND OUT."

"What is your husband's name?"

"WILLIAM, BILL."

"What is his job?"

"WORK'S WITH HORSES."

"Do you know where you live?"

"JUST OUTSIDE LONDON."

"How are your children?"

"LITTLE GIRL IS JUST WALKING, HUSBAND KILLED ME."

"How?"

"HE KEPT HITTING ME, KILLED ME. VERY ANGRY. WHO'S LOOKING AFTER MY CHILDREN?"

(At this stage Gail was very distressed so I decided to take her forward to her next life.)

"What is the year?"

"1912."

"Who are you?"

"A LITTLE GIRL, FEEL HAPPY...LOOKING FOR MUM AND DAD. FOUND MUM CAN'T FIND DAD."

"What is your mum's name?"

"PETRA."

"When were you born?"

"BORN 1907."

"What's your name?"

"PETRA, SAME AS MY MUM'S. MY DAD'S DEAD. DAD WAS OLD. I'M A SECRET FROM DAD'S FAMILY."

"What does your mum look like?"

"MUM HAS BLOND HAIR, WAVES, EVERYTHING MAKES ME LAUGH."

"What country do you live in?"

"HOLLAND."

"I want to move you forward now Petra, you are now at your thirteenth birthday, what do you see?"

"MY UNCLE ALF, HE IS MY MUM'S BROTHER, TALL, HIS EYE'S SMILING, I PLAY WITH HIM."

"What is Alf wearing?"

"DARK UNIFORM TWO ROWS OF BUTTONS, HE DOESN'T ALWAYS WEAR UNIFORM."

"What does Alf look like?"

"TALL, DARK HAIR, WHISKERS ON HIS FACE. MAKES ME LAUGH. PICKS ME UP MOVES HIS WHISKERS UP AND DOWN NECK."

"ALF PLAYS WITH ME IN THE FIELD. I FEED THE HORSES."

"HE HAS TWO HORSES. FRIGHTENED FAR TOO BIG. ONLY RIDE WHEN ALF IS THERE."

"Petra can you tell me how your hair looks?"

"LONG BLOND."

"Where are you now?"

"IN THE FIELD."

"Are you with the horses?"

"YES I'M FEEDING THEM, THERE IS SOMEONE WATCHING ME."

"Who?"

"HE PICKS GRASS AND CHEWS IT."

"Who is he?"

"NOT SPOKEN WITH HIM."

"What is he wearing?"

"WHITE SHIRT, HANDSOME. MY UNCLE ALF IS VERY PROTECTIVE OF ME, LOVE MY UNCLE."

"I'm going to move you forward, your now twenty five years old."

"Where are you?"

"AT HOME."

"Who is with you?"

"EDWARD, UNCLE ALF NOT PLEASED."

"Is anyone else with you?"

"YES."

"Could you tell me who?"

"ROBERT."

"Who is Robert?"

"HE IS MY BABY ROBBIE, CHUBBY FACE MAKES ME SMILE."

"Who is the father?"

"EDWARD."

"Do you love him?"

"YES AND HE LOVES ME, BUT HE COMES AND GOES, I DO LOVE HIM."

"I'm now going to move you forward to the time you went over to spirit, how old are you?"

"THIRTY-FIVE"

"Are Edward and Robbie still with you?"

"YES."

"Do you have any more children?"

"NO"

"WISH UNCLE ALF COULD SEE ROBBIE, HE DIED, ROBBIE LOOKS JUST LIKE HIM."

"How is Edward?"

"NOT GOOD HE DOESN'T LIKE ME, HE GOES WITH OTHER WOMEN. NO GOOD TO ME. SCARED NOBODY WILL LOOK AFTER ROBBIE."

"Why?"

"I'M DYING T. B. BAD CHEST, SO SCARED DON'T WANT TO LEAVE ROBBIE."

At this stage I bring Gail out of her trance but before she leaves she tries to hold onto Robbie. I bring her out. The session has lasted just over an hour and a half.

The session has revealed why Gail has a fear of leaving her son in this life time and the fact she has died young twice in her past two incarnations, once at the hand of her partner.

In her current life her partner was abusive but more with threats and intimidation rather than psychical violence.

The one big difference being he had died young this time around leaving Gail to pick up the pieces. Whereas in the previous lives Gail was the one who had died.

I believe she now has a chance to rebuild the life she should have with her son. Only time will tell if will be successful, but if she draws on the knowledge she now possesses it will help her conquer the innermost fears that lie deep down.

There is no conclusion to Gail's story at the moment because hers is a real life and she is living through what is an ever-changing time. But, as I said at the beginning she will always be my friend.

Another man who I helped was so afraid of flying he would rather cross the Atlantic by boat than get on a plane. He lived in America and his family in the UK. He made the long journey to see his parent's brothers and sister yearly. If he could fly on a plane, life would be much easier. But his phobia held him in a stranglehold; he was petrified with irrational fear at the thought of flying.

We are born with two fears or phobias: fear of water and fear of heights. It's normal to have these natural fears. It goes back to the time when we needed to survive. If we fell into water or leaped off a cliff top we would die. So inborn phobias serve a common purpose. Without them the human race would not have evolved so fast. All other fears are either learned behavior such as, being stung by a wasp as a child taught us to fear wasps. If something from a Past Life is locked deep in our memories, regression though hypnosis is needed to access the fear.

During Past Life regression I believe we access our Cell Memory. This is our personal memory of everything we ever experienced through every life we lived. This record is stored in the DNA of every cell in our bodies; a record of all the knowledge and lessons that life taught us throughout our existence. Soul memory, which is deeper set, is the memory of life between lives. It is our record of what happens to us while in spirit.

This man was in genuine need of help. His fears were real to the extent that he had altered his life to avoid dealing with the situation. He was prepared to do whatever it took to rid him of this paralyzing condition.

My voice softly echoed around the small room, "I want you to focus only on my voice, I don't want you to do anything except relax." I began, "Close your eyes and trust in my voice to guide you."

I had done this a hundred times before. I could sense the man sinking down further until he was deep under the hypnotic trance. Now I could regress him stage by stage; first through his current life, back through school, childhood, his memories of growing up came flooding back, with a tide of emotion, one minute laughing, the next crying, moving along at a pace going back further. He was four years old, two years old, one, then back to his earliest memories in his mother womb, warm peaceful. I could see he was at ease with the process. This was enough for his first time this deep under. I brought him back up through the same stages until he was back in the room with me. I never take a client back into a previous life too soon, especially if they have never experienced hypnosis. People have different reactions and I always like to see how they feel when coming out. Past Life memories can be upsetting and the last thing I want is a disoriented person with emotional fears surfacing for the first time in many years being sent out into the world to deal with their everyday routine alone.

A week later the man returned. This time I could see he was looking forward to the session. He was more relaxed, ready to explore whatever I could uncover from his deep subconscious memory.

He was under very soon, knowing what to expect helps. The difference this time was he would be going back past this lifetime. I knew it was the fear of flying that had brought him to me and he had just turned thirty-one. This gave me a time period of about fifty years to work with, since the first flight by the Wright brothers was in 1912, I knew this phobia was going to be based in a lifetime that fell between those years. Starting step by step I gradually moved him back in time (in Past Life regression "time" is the only indicator that people can relate to). "I would like you to step back let your mind guide your thoughts." I could sense him tensing up.

"Tell me what you are feeling."

His voice was shallow and a bit hard to hear. He started with, "I'm flying, so much noise, I can hardly hear myself think.

"How are you flying?"

"Airplane."

"Can you describe the airplane you're in?"

"Small with square wings, glass above my head, it's a fighter, a World War Two fighter"

"What are you wearing?"

I felt him look down at himself almost in disbelief. He described the uniform of an American fighter pilot right down to the handgun and knife he wore in his flight suit. Other information followed; his name, rank and squadron. This was good because now we had the information we needed to verify this person actually lived and wasn't a fantasy brought on by watching too many World War II movies. I brought him out of his trance. I didn't want him to relive the one thing he feared, it wasn't necessary. Research would fill in the missing pieces. He was under for well over two hours and sessions usually last an hour or less. Because we become over-tired this was an exception. The evidence he provided was beyond belief. I had to follow up the story. But where to start? No better place than the service records of the U.S. Air Force.

There was a photograph of a fresh young man with his service number. It transpired that he was shot down and killed over the Atlantic! He was twenty-two when he died. He flew Mustangs, a square winged fighter aircraft. The date of his death was October 15 1943. Amazing proof of a life he had lived some thirty years before being born again into an English family.

That year, I had an emotional feeling when we visited the American War Cemetery to pay tribute to this young man who was shot down defending his country. He traced the family to Alabama where they still lived. While his parents had died, his brother and two sisters, now in their sixty's, and their children and grand children all attended.

I still get letters from him from time to time telling me that he flies without fear. He has two homes; one in America and one in England.

Seeing is believing. I always want to experience things. Without experience you can listen to others and relate to the teachings but you never truly know completely. All you can do is trust second-hand feelings when things you know with all your heart are opposites. I was told the next two stories about Past Life regression so they are second hand. I can't vouch for them personally. Having said that, they are very interesting. They are similar to the American Pilot's experience and come from a source that I trust.

A small child in India knew far too much about his previous lifetime. From the age of five the boy was convinced that he had owned a television shop in a city many miles from where he lived now. What made this story stand out was this: In his account he had been shot three times in the chest and the boy's chest has three round birth marks the shape and size a bullet would make. Birthmarks are often clues to how we might have died. In this child's case the details of his past life were remarkable. He knew his wife's name and their children's names. He also describes the front and insides of the shop in great detail. His mother and father didn't believe him. How could their special little boy have been a completely different person in another life that was recent enough for him to remember everything? As the boy grew he felt compelled to visit the city where he knew he had lived and find his shop. He did this to the surprise of both his new and old families.

The outcome was that he was able to convince his wife and children who he really was. He now runs that shop! This is a very remarkable story but I've learned that Past Life stories often are.

The second story is that of a man who lived in Canada in the 1970's. He was an antiques dealer, with a love of timepieces, clocks, and coins. One particular clock, a large old gold and diamond carriage clock had caught his eye in the window of a local jewelers. He felt like it was familiar yet how could that be? The clock must be well over ninety years old. He looked but he knew the price was way beyond what he could afford. The man went about his normal daily routine but just couldn't get the carriage clock out of his thoughts. He dreamt about it, strange dreams where he was sitting around a table with people he had never seen before. They were celebrating, the room was dimly lit with lots of old pictures on the walls, and the gold diamond carriage clock was on the mantelpiece above the fire. Was he going mad he asked himself? This dream was constant and the people became like real figures in his mind. Everyday as he walked past the shop, the clock sat there looking at him, quietly ticking away, drawing his attention like it had hypnotic power.

By the time he went to his doctor, his life was being taken over by clear visions of another time and place. His doctor wasn't sure what he could do for him, but he knew a colleague who specialized in Past Life regression. Through a series of events he was sitting in my office being taken deep into a trance.

He was in the room he saw in his visions; a large oblong room with a large dining table. He was a young man about fourteen years old. His whole family surrounded him, on his head was a small cap (kippah). He was Jewish as was his whole family. Looking around the room he saw it was filled with valuable antiques and on the mantelpiece was a gold and diamond carriage clock dimly lit in the flicking gaslight.

The scene changed. He was now in his early twenties dressed in rags, painfully thin, no sign of his family, watching in horror as bodies were being thrown and kicked into a large trench. He felt a sharp pain, then falling, falling so far, then the feeling of freedom, his last memories were of watching the souls of hundreds of people escaping upwards like fireflies being released from a jar.

He had lived before. The clock was a trigger to unlock these memories of a life as a Jewish man who died in the Holocaust.

The story goes that after being regressed he told his remarkable experience to the owner of the jewelry shop who gave him back the clock. If true, a fitting end.

This convinced me that Past Lives really do have an effect on our current life. It's a progression of understanding, free will, fate and sometimes destiny that guides our very soul's existence.

My own Past Life regression reinforced my understanding of the subject. While studying I was given the opportunity to be taken back through a Past Life. Never being shy or one to turn down a chance to learn something new about myself, I knew I had to do this.

I remember thinking you've got your work cut out with me! Then I was under; awake but not awake, going back through my life, feeling the emotion of childhood, sitting in the doctor's waiting room, watching Katie run across the road, the fear of the footsteps outside my bedroom window, I felt very alone. Then I moved backwards into a warm safe feeling.

I heard a voice pushing me back and back. "Where are you now it asked?"

I'm standing in a field. I looked down and saw I was dressed in heavy brown trousers, with braces, light blue shirt, and a cap. I was a farmer; it was early spring, the year 1912. To the amazement of my teacher I was speaking French (a language of which I had no previous knowledge.) So I was a French farmer in 1912.

"I want to take you forward to the moment just before you passed into spirit. Where are you?"

I was in a trench. The year was 1917. I was wearing the uniform of a French solider, I was about to be bayoneted in the throat (even in this life my throat is my weak point). I was killed in the battle for Epees on the French Belgium border.

Like all good Past Life regressions, the impressions given must be verified. Everything that came out that day was backed up with facts, even my name Dominique.

So far I have shown impressive evidence on Past Life regression. But what if we could go forward; to Future Live Progression. You already know my thoughts are that time is a manmade structure that we use to order our lives.

Who says what time is? We turn the clocks back and forward each year and every fourth year we gain a whole day! What's that all about? It just goes to show how we manipulate time for our own ends.

Take this a step further. If time has no beginning or end it makes it a circle. So if we can go back in time then we can also go forward. That's where Future Life Progression fits into the bigger picture. Now imagine going forward in your own life. What would you like to know? It's a good question because if we know what's coming up we can deal with problems before they arise and life is no longer beyond your control. That's only on a personal level. Let's think about Future Life Progression on a world level. We are dealing with real big issues. Imagine what it would be like to take a glimpse at what the planet will be like in a hundred years. The fact that we can move forward is a positive message. In my personal experience of progression the people on Earth have learned to adapt to the ever-changing climate, homes are built underground, cars run on water, we get free energy from natural sources, microbes eat rubbish, algae soak up pollution. We have a bright future as a race. We have always faced up to changes needed to survive; the future is no different.

So what can past or future lives teach us? In a word; survival. The fact is that the soul is eternal and every one of us accountable for our own actions. How we live, what we say, and making right or wrong choices. We are here to learn. Life isn't set out in front of us. We all have free will. We can do as we wish; I find it too hard to believe that a greater force controls our lives.

Having said that, the choices we make start before we are born. Pathways we wish to follow, experiences we choose to take are all decided before we start our new life. These will be placed along our journey if we decide to choose to take that pathway. When we pass over into the spirit world we are judged but only by ourselves. We all have our personal journeys. Some will take the quick route; others will decide to take a slower pace. So whichever way we decided to play our time out here on Earth, it pays to think positive and face difficulties knowing that at some point we will overcome and move on, if not in our current life maybe in the next one.

One subject I haven't covered in this chapter so far is Shamanism. For centuries all over the world, shaman have experienced personal life journeys with the help of a natural drug called Iowasca.

Iowasca is two different plants that are brought together; the root of one and the leaves of another. When combined and boiled together in water they make a rich black tea which can be drunk. It tastes of bitter licorice. You are recommended not to eat for twenty-four hours before you drink it because if you have food in your system the Iowasca will clear your body of that food before it starts you on your journey.

I have heard many stories by many people of their Iowasca journeys. People have met strange creatures that healed bad backs, broken limbs and so on. Since I have never experienced these beings for myself, I keep an open mind on these claims. But I have been taken forward into a time and place I couldn't explain that made me face my own fears. This is what happened.

I knew I wanted to do this. I had read much about Iowasca with others explaining how it had changed their life through a journey into the subconscious mind. A good friend told me to relax while going where my journey took me. I made sure nobody would bother me for the next few hours. I took the phone off the hook, drew the curtains and swallowed a whole mug of tepid bitter black liquid in one gulp. I felt sick; my head was spinning, my mouth dry and rough. I had expected all these feelings so I relaxed and made sure my body was in a comfortable position. I lay down and closed my eyes. At this stage I had no sense of time so I don't know how long it was before I felt a dream-like state around my thoughts. I was in the desert, jet planes were flying all around me. I watched in horror as one plane was shot out of the air, black smoke billowed from the aircraft, the pilot was thrown into the air, then drifting down slowly, his pale blue parachute silent in the still air. The noise was loud, people shouting and firing guns into the air in celebration.

I was with a group of men, soldiers by the way they were dressed. I was living this experience as though I had always been in this life. I slept, ate and drank with the other men. We lived in an underground bunker built into the sand with blocks of stone and iron windows and doors. I was fighting another war but this time I was myself in the desert.

It was night now. I settled down in a metal-framed bunk bed to get some rest. I felt uneasy, the air was tense and dry, the other men on edge. I heard loud explosions going off in the distance, jet planes roared overhead. I was scared. Then I heard a loud bang and shouting. I saw a man I didn't recognize. I felt like my head was hit by a large fist; then I came to, I was back in my room the sunlight shining though the gap in my curtains. I felt disorientated, my eyes couldn't focus, my head painful, my arms and legs stiff. I glanced towards my clock, it was ten o'clock. I had been under for over twelve hours!

What had I experienced? I think I had seen my own death in this life. If ever there was a war in the desert I would make sure I was well away from it I told myself. It was the summer of 1984 the first Gulf war was only six years away.

Looking back I believe what I saw was the end of my life. It was my biggest fear. I also believe that the knowledge I gained saved my life, because I knew if I ever saw that bunker I would do all I could to escape

Chapter Four

The Circle of life

My head sometimes fills with so many questions I feel it will burst wide open! My guide and mentor Red Cloud always answers my questions with another two. He told me that I already have all the answers deep down in my soul. Everything that ever has been or ever will be is with you. So to find the answers to any question we must look deep inside, trusting what we find.

One question that has cost me many hours of searching is; how are souls created?

I have meditated on this question many times. Here are my conclusions.

Everything in the universe is energy without exception; from the star that lights and warms our planet to the very thoughts that we give out.

Our souls are formed from this energy that surrounds our existence. It's very simple. The reason the answers are always deep inside is because we are made up from the energy that created by those thoughts.

Thoughts are powerful. Thoughts of love, which is the one and only universal law (love is everything) connects us with every thing that was and everything that is.

So our souls are born from concentrated universal energy that is; love. Everyone of us has that love spark so as the soul starts its journey as a brand new life-form the energy is pure unaffected by life's ups and downs before it is placed in a mortal body. I have been shown the birth of new souls during meditation. It's a wonderful emotional experience, something we as humans would find hard to comprehend. We are such a small part of the universe.

From our very first step our souls soak up every human experience. The energy all around us contains the universal knowledge or claircognizance. We can all tap into this source of knowledge and contribute to it. When we send our thoughts out either in the form of questions or by working out the answers (soul searching] we are adding to the sum of knowledge so others can benefit.

Positive thought is very important in order to function. We are the thoughts we think. In the spirit world I believe we are divided by thoughts. This took me some time to work out, but it explains the order of understanding. Each life we are given is an opportunity to progress but we can only progress by learning. This process is started by thought. In spirit thoughts control everything. So if we learn to think negative thoughts while living our human lives then, in spirit, we will still think the same way; hence we will be bogged down with worries and create our own private hell. How many people do you meet who are so stuck in their own negative thoughts that they can't see the positive side of how wonderful life is?

There are other people who think they can do anything. These people have a positive attitude not just to life but to their very existence; coming across difficult decisions spurs them on to find the right answers by listening to inner self or the universal knowledge. They are open enough to ask questions, while searching for answers that can be justified not just accepted.

Red Cloud explains this to me by saying, "Anyone can follow the crowd."

Your spirit body is only limited by how you think. Your imagination is the key to unlock a whole universe of possibilities so why block yourself?

As your soul travels along its journey to achieve perfection and return to pure energy (the circle of life] we have much to experience, learn and achieve.

We don't have to live our lives alone; we have a choice. Deciding who will be with us is a lottery, or is it? Are we drawn to some rather than others because we have a soul connection? What could it possible mean? Do the people we think we have chosen by free will turn out to be souls who have traveled through many life times at our side? Just thinking about whether or not we have free will is enough to blow my mind wide open. So let's look at soul connections.

This is what I have come to believe. The soul is like an orange. It has eleven segments; each person has one segment of a soul within them (light spark]. The other ten segments are either in spirit or in a mortal body. If we come across another person with the same spark it is like finding yourself, your soul mate. The feelings are very strong emotionally; a sense of comfort, knowing someone else feels the same way without knowing why. Soul mates are drawn to one another for many reasons. To help each other learn certain life lessons, to bring other souls into this mortal world, even to leave the other partner with problems beyond belief (Gail's Story Chapter 3]. But overall soul mate relationships can be very hard work, not for the faint hearted.

When people ask me if they will ever find their soul mate, I often think in private "If it's meant to be it doesn't matter were you are they will find you".

I'm reminded of the lady from Scotland on holiday in Australia. As she walked along the beach she was hit by a large wave of emotion as she walked past the fishing boats. The man tying his nets together looked very familiar. She was worried about his safety but why? She had no idea who he was. He was very attractive so she stopped and started a conversation never telling him of the strange bond she felt for him, a man twelve thousand miles away from home. The meeting was pure chance but the more he talked the more she recognized this man. One thing lead to another and an affair started. Over the next few months they fell in love but she always knew deep down that he would leave her. She felt dread when he went to sea in his fishing boat and became very possessive, He couldn't cope with the way she became so the relationship failed. She moved back to Scotland looking for answers to why she had gone through such an experience. I remember her saying to me, "I thought he was my soul mate."

She was right; this man was her soul mate. When I took her back there he was, about to go off to war. He left her and their three children. Needless to say he never came back.

Soul mates don't have to be partners; they can be mother and child, cousins, two people of the same sex, brother and sister, the list is endless.

So be careful what you wish for. You never know you just might find it anything is possible when it comes to soul mates!

Young souls and Old souls are expressions we are used to hearing. What is meant by what on the surface are throwaway lines we use to describe our children?

Young souls I've touched on. They are pure of thought, a blank canvas where the influence of others becomes the beginning of their understanding. In the past I have regressed such people finding very little stored in either the cell memory or soul memory. I find these souls normally have their life path shown to them before they start a human journey. This helps them understand the purpose while allowing for free will. No soul would ever be made to do anything having just been shown the benefits of going through an experience.

Old souls: Red Cloud my mentor and guide told me early on in my life that I had had many faces! I don't think he was trying to insult me just get across the many lifetimes I had lived. As a human it's hard to comprehend the knowledge that being a part of many different cultures, languages, sexes, every lifetime lived was for a purpose. When a mother looks at a child and sees knowledge and wisdom in their eyes it's easy to see where the expression comes from. Even if they're not sure what's being said, it has enormous implications. The feeling of holding a brand new baby is beyond words, looking into a child's eyes can help you see so much. I swear that when my first son was born and his blue eyes opened wide, I saw his life going before my eyes like a DVD on fast forward. I'm sure those of you who are parents have experienced a similar sensation. Being a parent is a special part of anyone's life. Having the knowledge that the soul of that child chose you to guide them through the beginning of their life is special. Once you have this realization the little problems life throws up seem to be insignificant.

Old souls are normally teachers; souls that have learned many lessons and have agreed to be reborn to help others, while coping with the day-to-day trials of living a human existence. A person who is an Old soul is special. It means their understanding of purpose is greater, being able to see past as well as present.

With the concept of the soul also comes order. As we live through each life we store a record of that life in our cell memory, a blue print of every action whether good or bad. In some religions this is know as karma. What we should know is that we stand alone, accountable. I have regressed people who stayed in the same loop for many life times, making the same mistakes, choosing to return to try and leap that particular hurdle.

When I look back at my own life I know the hurdles I had to jump. First were my parents. I choose who they were to be and I certainly didn't make an easy choice. But without putting myself in that position, the lessons I learned growing up wouldn't have made me strong enough to become the person I am today. School was also a test. Moving away from my friends at a young age meant I had to learn to make new friends.

With all this in mind do we have free will? Let's go back to the beginning before we start a new life. Do we have free will in choosing who our parents are going to be? The answer is no. Let me explain. Each soul group has its own teachers or mentors; this group is known as The Council of Elders. My Elders consist of seven men. Other groups of Elders can have a mixture of males, females, or even all females so there is no fixed formula. We must present the journey we should take in our next incarnation before them after reviewing previous life times. In other words, we are guided by our personal Elders but we make the final choice. In no way is this free will; its free choice from a selection of options. It's like being told you can vote for anyone you like as long as their name is on the list.

The parent or parents we choose are the best ones shown to us for what we need to experience in the first part of our human life; still no free will. Yes, we have the choice given to us by our Elders.

Now we're born, starting all over again. Our parents now have total influence over our life while we grow. The food we eat, the clothes we wear, where we live, whether rich or poor. As we get older they decide the education we receive. Do we have free will in any of these situations? No way. As adults we carry with us all the teachings and influences passed on by everyone who has crossed our path. Now we can make decisions for our self based on the person we have become.

Our lives are based on the choices we are given to make. Making the right choices takes us down the fast route. Making the wrong decisions slows our progress. It's only if we don't make choices that we stand still.

If free will means doing nothing, then we can choose to stand still. This may account for why we need to live so many lifetimes. I'm still waiting to meet the prefect person. The fact that we are here at this moment means we still have lessons to learn. The secret is finding out what those lesson's are and who our teachers will be.

Before I move on to the next subject, I would like to leave you with two thoughts on free will. Think back to how and when you met your partner or, if you haven't met that special person yet, think of all the people that you have met in your lifetime; why them? Why did you choose to move past some persons? It's worth a few moments of consideration. When you have thought about that consider where your thoughts come from. Are the thoughts you think all yours or do they come from a number of sources, mentors and guides, past and future selves, people you live and work with or even through dreams? Now there's a thought!

Everything in life has a beginning, middle, and end. We are born, we live, and then die. It's very simple when we think about life in this way, apart from one thing; we never die. We leave one existence for another.

I think about death as uncorking the bottle, releasing the soul energy, the body is an empty vessel after the life force has been set free. I was asked a very interesting question about the point of passing recently. A lady's sister was taken ill very suddenly, suffered a stroke that almost killed her but the doctors had managed to save her life. Now she was in a coma, unable to breath by herself, on a life support machine. The family was distraught with worry, what were they to do? Should they accept the death of a person they loved very much, or hope that she might make it and be back to normal or should they switch the machine off and accept that she was gone?

I was explaining how I believed that as soon as the body stopped functioning the soul was released to the lady. Right then, someone with a deep Irish accent inside my head said, "Tell her I'm here," the voice demanded. It said, "It's me Cathy."

I could hear the voice of my Guide Red Cloud "trust."

O. K I thought here goes, "Was your sisters name Cathy?" I asked.

Thud. The phone dropped. "My God how did you know that?" The voice was shaking. I could hear tears, her voice lowered, "Are you sure it's Cathy?"

"Yes."

A lady stood in front of my mind. It could only be her sister. She wasn't lying in a hospital bed on a life support machine; she was in spirit, desperate to get though to her family.

I passed on some other messages for her husband, children and friends and said good bye knowing that now the family could let go and turn off the life support knowing that their mother, wife, friend and sister had gone.

We accept that death is only change but do we decide on how we pass over? When working with Past Life regression I have found that the soul is released just before the point of transformation. People have described how they watched the circumstances of their last moments. It was like watching a film of an old friend, we become very attached to our body. In Chapter 2 on Past Lives you will remember the story of the World War II fighter pilot as he described in graphic detail during his regression watching himself going down in flames. Although he felt the fear, emotion, and pain he said it was surreal.

When people pass over while young, due to war, accidents and even suicide, they have missed the opportunity to live out their full potential. Whether or not their life was meant to end the way it did, I'm not sure if circumstance, or fate, plays a part. In my own life I'm sure I would have died in the first Gulf War if I hadn't taken notice of what I experienced while on my Iowasca journey. So you can change, but only if you become aware. There are no short cuts that prevent you from going through certain events. If life gets tough and you decide to take your own life, you will face the same problems again in your next life and your next until you learn to overcome the difficulties.

During Past Life regressions many of the cases I examined are of people who died young in their last life. It seems that if you pass into spirit because of someone else or an accident, suicide, or illness, you're more likely to move onto your next life soon. I think this sometimes short circuits the process souls go through in wiping their cell and soul memory (moving past memory beyond our conscious thoughts] leaving thoughts and memories close to the surface in the new incarnation. The story of the little boy from India is a prime example. This can leave us with fears; phobias, even birthmarks that we can't explain in our current lives.

I met one such lady. She had two signs of being brought back too soon leaving her with memories that weren't hers.

As a hypnotist and therapist I meet many people with phobias; some rational, some not. I knew right away that this lady was one for whom phobias were real and not learned behavior. (When we fear something it's because it happened to us in this lifetime.)

She was a very attractive, petite, neat person. She was well dressed and spoken. She had a dark purple port-wine stain or dark birthmark above her left eye. She knew I noticed it as she caught my glance. She made no attempt to cover it up with makeup but I could see how it made her feel.

I smiled and asked her to sit in the deep comfy chair which seemed to swallow her. "How can I help?"

Her voice was warm and friendly, "I hope you can help. I've come to see you because I can't cope anymore." she paused, "It's birds .I can't get rid of this fear I have. It's affecting my life so much I can hardly walk outside my house."

I could see she was getting upset but I also knew that if the answer were inside her we would find it together. I explained how I would take her back through her subconscious mind to see what laid beneath the surface.

Phobias can be buried deep inside. It can take weeks, sometimes months to find the right memory. Over the next few weeks I got used to her visits slowly making progress backwards. Her previous lives had been normal, nothing about birds.

Then we hit on why. She described feeling hot, thirsty; her skin was dark coffee colored, and a piece of what she described as leather was around her waist. She was walking in the desert; big red rocks surrounded her, she felt exhausted, and then saw a huge bird come straight at her. That was it. The screen went black. She felt clam and peaceful, no longer tried or thirsty. I could bring her out now knowing where the phobia had its roots. Over the next two sessions we explored this past life.

65

She had lived in the outback in Australia. Her death was caused by dehydration; her last memory of that lifetime was being attack by a large bird that pecked her left eye out! No wonder she had a fear of birds. Everyday she was reminded of that experience in her subconscious when she looked in the mirror.

The work we did together changed her life. It took just over four months. Taking sixteen weeks out of a lifetime and finding peace of mind from being brave enough to face her fears was well worth every minute.

We may never realize that we have a phobia until we come across a situation that triggers the fear. This can be alarming if it is a surprise we didn't suspect.

Imagine how a man felt when he had to face his worst fear. It was left over from a lifetime that was cut short and he had no prior knowledge.

People in trouble find their way to my door. I am often the last point of call after trying many other solutions. So when a man knocked at my door with panic in his body language, I knew he was looking for answers that he could not find in his logical world. "You have to be able to help me."

These words, that I hear often, causes my heart to sink knowing that if I can't find the answers this person is going to be stuck.

I sat him down in my big armchair and waited for him to explain "Please start at the beginning," I urged.

"I can't walk up stairs." the man blurted out almost embarrassed to admit or speak the words.

I had learned not to be judgmental but I had never come across a person who had a phobia over stairs.

He continued, "About three months ago my life was fantastic. I had just landed my dream job working in London, I couldn't wait to get started." He paused, then moved forward in the chair, "It's the underground. I just can't use the escalators. I have a real fear of climbing up from the bottom. I freeze like I'm going to die."

Now he had my full attention. Could this be learned behavior? Had he fallen down at some stage during his lifetime? Even if he had, this wouldn't fit because he couldn't climb stairs without going into a panic.

I found myself saying in a reassured manner, "It'll be alright. I'm sure this is something left from a previous life," whether or not it was, we were going to find out.

"I want you to listen to my voice and my voice only." I began.

It was only his second session, the first one had been a challenge. This time he was at ease and went under quickly. It turned out he had been a sheep rustler, stealing for a living. He talked about this far away life as if he was living back in Wales. He described the landscape, his family, even the food he ate that day. Taking him forward step by step to the time of his death, he became very frightened. He described walking into a stone building with two floors. It was a courtroom, he was on trial, accused of stealing sheep. He was found guilty and at this stage I had to calm him down. He was panicking. In front of him was a steep wooden staircase that wound up to the second floor. He was forced to climb it. On reaching the top a noose was placed around his neck and he was pushed over the edge and hung in the stairwell. It was horrific, I had to let him relive the experience so he could realize that his fear of steep staircases had been imbedded into his subconscious and the London underground had unearthed this long forgotten memory.

By the time he recovered enough to stand up I knew he would never be the same again. Past Life recall isn't always an easy thing to accept. Memories stirred up from long lost thoughts can change the way we view our current circumstances. This man was no exception. Once he worked out that the experience he had gone through was real, everything in his life moved forward at a tremendous pace. He now works for an ex-offender organization that deals with suicide. It's a long way away from his job in the city.

I think this last story is a prime example of someone who chose the wrong path and went the long way around to find his true calling. He didn't really make a choice; he was shown.

Being shown directions is not uncommon. We might not see it while we are stuck in testing. But our direction or purpose can open up once we face up to change. Spirit has a way of placing us in the position to face that change. It is either voluntary or it teaches us if we're unhappy that unhappiness will surface one way or another. It will eventually achieve the change and it will happen, the long way around.

The biggest change we ever make is moving from this life to the next. Many questions arise when we talk about passing into the spirit world.

So what happens when we leave this life behind?

One certain thing in living is that at some stage we will return home after going through the trials and tribulations living a human life has taught us. The spirit world is our true home so returning home is a cause for celebration; I have talked to people who were very surprised at the welcome they got. This was shown to me at a sitting I did.

As ever, the person had come hoping to receive a message from her late husband. She was a rather formal lady with strong religious beliefs, dressed in dark clothing, her voice somber. I sat her down and started to bring forward the pictures in my mind. Spirit has a way of teaching me lessons when I least expect. A man in his late sixty's stood in front of my mind; nothing remarkable about that, but what he was wearing made me sit up and check my vision. He wore a white toga, held a large glass of what looked like red wine, was certainly not sober and around his forehead were laurel leafs. His widow sitting across the table from me looking expectant; how do I explain this?

"I have your husband with me, he looks very well!" I found it hard to keep a straight face.

Apparently this lady, his wife for the last forty years, had kept a strong hold on him. He hadn't been able to break away from her strict regime; his life had been a dull existence. When he passed into spirit his family and friends who had gone before him decided to throw him a Roman Toga party! He was having the time of his spirit life! The thoughts he had for his wife weren't easy to pass on. As a medium I think you have a duty to give the message that you receive. If I had relayed this man's thoughts I'm sure her reaction would have been one of surprise or even horror. I was so pleased that I could reassure her that her husband had never looked better. And I was pleased that she could not read my thoughts that day! Another lesson: To be a medium you need the skills of a diplomat. Thought is so very powerful.

To grasp this concept we have to think like spiritual beings not human beings with our judgmental attitudes. We are conditioned to love or hate extremes. The order of life in the spirit world is dictated by thought; we create the welcome at our passing. If our mind is full of hate, lost opportunities and fear we create this in our spirit world, our passing being part of the learning experience. When we talk about lost souls I think we are talking about souls who haven't learned to be positive or can't except events or do not yet realize that their energy has changed from human to spirit. These souls can be lost forever in a sea of despair. Only positive thought can rescue a soul trapped in this position. (I discuss trapped spirits in the next chapter.) Do we choose the time place and how we pass into spirit? Again the answer is simple. You don't have to look past personal responsibility. Our life span is around seventy-five years. We can take away years from this human time limit by life style. The food we choose, do we exercise? Smoke? Drink? Take mood-changing drugs? The list is endless, we all have choices but a lifetime as a human is up to us. The longer we live the more we learn; the more we can teach others. I'll address one exception and that is accidental passing. Yes, I do feel that life can change in an instant but through my experience of Past Life regression I have discovered the lives that come back within months of passing are those who were stopped in their tracks early for whatever reason.

The normal life span in the 1500's was only around forty years. In a hundred years time I have no doubt our human life span will reach well over a century given the advances we have in medicines. But this still won't stop the fact that people pass over young and the longer you live the more you learn. I also believe that as a soul we have to experience many situations including what it's like to pass by many different methods.

I have often heard "I'm not scared of death but I'm scared of how I might die."

Because life is eternal you never die, it's just a transformation. I believe we have to learn about these transformations and the only way is experience. Each day that we live in this world is a blessing. It teaches us something money can't buy; wisdom and knowledge. Looking at the place we are going to be when we pass is more of a challenge. Whether or not we have any control on this is pure speculation. Our lives take many twists and turns and we are programmed to end up in a certain part of the world before we pass. I doubt this very much. I would go more with choice; not always ours but that of others we choose to live along side. The spirit world is all around us; a dimension that vibrates at a different frequency, a world within a world, the same but different. Personal choice and how we think plays a part in when we move over to spirit. Negative thought can lead us down the wrong pathways. Suicide is a state of mind.

Our thoughts can put us in a place within yourself which means the only way out is to let go. Every instinct we are born with fights these feelings for a good reason. We have chosen to place ourselves in this position. If we don't face it the chances are that we will have to relive that same situation the next lifetime round. It is easy to get stuck in a loop. There is no easy way out.

So how do we make the choice? How is it up to what we and others need to experience in order to progress? I think back to how my father's life ended, his one selfless experience affected many others.

Also, there is Katie, my school friend who was knocked over by a lorry. Try as I might I can't remember any of my other friends of that time by name. Katie stays with me even now; her personal sacrifice convinced me I should work with spirit. What if Katie had taken a different turn that September day? I would have still worked with spirits as my granddad George would have pushed me in that direction but it would have taken longer.

Our true calling is never straightforward. What we do with our lives is up to us. We have choice. I also believe we have certain lessons to learn in every life we live. I don't believe in fate. We make our choices from what we are given. Think positive as this helps you every day of your life; not only in the human form, but also when we return home to spirit.

As Red Cloud tells me "Everything that ever was is. Everything that every shall be has been."

Chapter Five

Passageway

I don't believe in the paranormal. There are things in this universe that we don't understand, but that doesn't make them paranormal. When people talk about the supernatural, I don't take much notice. I would rather experience it first hand. Over the years my personal search has taken me far and wide looking to experience different "paranormal activity." I have explored countless buildings; most have nothing of note. I have lost count of pubs that claim to have a resident ghost. To me ghosts are sentient, trapped souls. If you come across them you should do everything in your power to help them move over to the spirit world.

Red Cloud asked me the question "How would you like to be trapped in time with no way out?"

I must admit living the same day over and over again has little appeal to me. So when I come across a house with a ghost all I think is, how cruel.

But the question arises. How does a soul become trapped? Normally it is through fear; our thoughts can hold us in one place. At the moment the soul is released, if it's unexpected or the person has a deep attachment to another person, then the soul doesn't become aware of the spirit world or the passageway in between. It's straightforward. They never see the light. So their existence stays the same but without human form. I have come across souls that were in the same place for hundreds of years; time just stands still for them. They are often unaware of any fuss they cause. The first thing I attempt is to make contact very carefully; ask their name, the year, offer a few reassurances, show no hostile intent, allow them to see their plight without pushing too hard. It's rather like trying to feed a timid animal. I offer the exit slowly sending out thoughts of love. I carry on the conversation while holding onto the vision of the passageway between the two worlds. I've spent whole days where time was unimportant in coaxing spirits towards the home world. Being able to show them the light is a gift. It means they can continue their soul journey often being reborn very quickly once returning home to the spirit world.

If you ever come across a trapped soul don't hide the fact. Help them. It could be you in another life.

Replay ghosts are fantastic. I love finding a road or a house that has a replay ghost. The spirit has long gone; you are watching a recording of the events. When a spirit is released the energy signature is very strong and can leave an imprint on the atmosphere. It's nature's way of recording history as it actually happened. First you must do your research. I know this might sound obvious but the most likely places we find replay ghosts is where someone else would have either stumbled upon the scene by accident or local legion has recorded the events. Once you establish your location, note any dates when ghosts were seen in the past. The key to watching these events is understanding how nature restarts the playback sequence. In my experience the calmer the weather the better. A long slow sequence of high pressure builds the electric current in the atmosphere; these are ideal conditions. Then you stake out and find the spot where the energy is at a high level. The temperature in these areas is normally lower so you don't have to rely on a medium being with you. A simple thermometer will point you in the right direction. Now focus your thoughts on the area. Then wait. To successfully see replay ghosts you must be patient. You might have to return to the same location on many occasions. Keep an eye on the weather conditions as this gives you the best chance of seeing a release of energy. It's nothing paranormal but very interesting to watch. Remember a slow buildup of high pressure in the area often activates the recording.

Not all ghosts are hard to find. Poltergeists are known for the way they draw attention to the fact that they are there. Hollywood movie directors show that these noises are usually mischievous but not malicious as if noisy ghosts are everywhere. They're not. There is usually a normal explanation when a building makes noise. A lady and daughter called me for help with their poltergeist. Their flat was perched on the top floor of a block of three rundown properties. I felt excited when ringing the doorbell. Could this be my chance to explore a real poltergeist? The lady was convinced she had a noisy ghost. Everyday at the same time it made the same sounds. I must say she was genuinely scared that this spirit had come for her twenty two year old daughter. I saw nothing outstanding as I walked up the dirty staircase; in the stairwell a black framed bike from the 1950's, an old vegetable rack and a smelly tray of cat litter. The harsh scent of bleach hit my nostrils. The contrast was total as I walked though the open front door to a small but beautifully arranged front room. Crystals adorned the mantle piece and shelves, a large black and white cat lay stretched out in front of the gas fire.

"That's Mr. Socks," the lady told me seeing he had drawn my glance. "Can I offer you a drink? Tea, coffee, beer?"

I declined feeling right at home. "Your ghost" I started, "you think you have a poltergeist?"

The woman nodded with reluctance.

"How often do you see it?" A very normal question in the circumstances.

"We have never seen it. But every morning and night we hear it. It makes a hell of a noise."

Well at least we have something to go on I thought; if it makes the same noise at the same times everyday I can wait and witness whatever this is. I've never known a prompt ghost but there is a first time for everything. I was intrigued.

"What time will you hear your poltergeist?" I ask

"About another twenty minutes."

"Then we have time for a cup of tea first then don't we?"

I have been in haunted locations that make the hairs on your head stand on end but this wasn't one of them. I felt right at home drinking my tea. I think I almost fell asleep because the next thing I heard was BANG, BANG followed by gurgling then lots of little bangs. Mr. Socks shot off his cozy resting place and hid behind the sofa.

"There you see!" shouted the lady pleased that her story was vindicated. "That's it. That's the ghost."

A huge smile came to my face. This poor lady had been scared stiff for months by her central heating system. There was air trapped in her pipes, not a poltergeist trapped in her house. That same evening I returned, not with my tape recorder but with a radiator key to bleed her heating system. I never heard from her or Mr. Socks again.

I have never come across a real noisy ghost. I've talked with people who have witnessed objects thrown across rooms and heard noises that they can't account for. But until I witness a poltergeist first hand I will keep an open mind.

One form of energy I can vouch for and have experienced first hand is that of a shadow ghost. This type of ghost hides in the corners of old buildings. The unique thing about a shadow ghost is that it's made up entirely from the negative thought energy of a soul that has passed over to spirit leaving behind this dark black negative energy. It was a very emotional encounter. Here's what happened.

It was great seeing everyone again. What with work and commitments I hadn't been able to take part in any investigations for well over a year. It was a small group, five in all, with one thing in common; seeking out the truth behind the so called paranormal through personal experience. We would travel the country looking for haunted locations in the hope of encountering ghosts. This particular building we discovered reportedly dated back to the eleventh century. So not only was I looking forward to sharing a long night with friends, I was excited in the prospect of exploring this old building.

The light was dimming by the time I finished walking around the house by myself. I always walked around alone first. This gave me a feel for the property and let me work out the best rooms for the nighttime visuals. On a ghost investigation nothing normally happens. You sit in one place for hours on end, cold, tried, and bored; it's not like you see on television programs. I've never carried a switched-on flashlight. The last thing you want to do is draw attention to yourself or disturb any spirit energy that might be there. If you did come across something you would sense it long before you saw it. So the quieter the better.

In this building I sensed two rooms that would be well worth exploring. We decided to split into two groups with one downstairs in the front room. This room felt friendly, a family room with the sound of children playing; the atmosphere was thick with spirit. It was the upstairs room that I was interested in. It was far darker; it felt more menacing with just an outside street lamp casting patches of orange light across the room at an angle. The two ladies with me were nervous as was I, but I've never been scared of anything I have come across. Without warning, the lady on my left starting crying; she sobbed uncontrollably. She told me later that a wave of emotion had gone right through her. She literally walked straight into a shadow ghost. As we watched a cloud of dark dust glided across the center of the floor and vanished into the recess behind the chimney. The room was dimly lit with the orange light but we all knew what we had witnessed. It was a shadow person. I had read of others encountering these very rare ghosts but never thought I would experience one first hand.

As a medium I'm used to being overwhelmed with emotional feelings but I felt nothing until I saw the dark cloud. My friend however got everything. Now that's what I call a personal experience. I waited in the room for the rest of the night but it never came back. The room went from menacing to restful in a period of two hours. I've been on hundreds of ghost investigations experiencing nothing other than a few orbs, but this one was well worth all the others put together. Because I now knew for sure that shadow ghosts are for real.

It wouldn't be long again before I encountered another shadow person. This time it was at Ghosthouse, a large Edwardian house, situated in the middle of England. The owners had experienced lots of strange occurrences. Replay ghosts seemed to appear at will and spirits of lost people would walk the along corridors between the eight large upstairs rooms. The cellar, while untouched, was especially interesting. The people who had bought the house a year earlier had set up web cams in all the rooms linking them to a website where anybody interested could sit and watch the ghostly activity and take snapshots of anything unusual. Every third month, the doors to the house were thrown open for anyone who wished to explore. This is where I came in. I took groups of interested people around, talking about the history, pointing out where the replay ghosts were seen. We held visuals in different rooms and a séance at midnight where I got the visitors involved if they wanted to contact the spirit world.

On one of the tours I chose to take a group of skeptical visitors to the cellar. It was pitch black apart from the light of the moon coming in through a top window. I wouldn't let anyone switch-on flashlights because if anything was down there I was going to find it. We had been sitting for a few moments when I felt it; the emotional feeling I experienced earlier that year. I knew we had something. When the lady next to me started getting upset but insisted she want to stay, my memory went back in my mind. There was no doubt that a shadow ghost was in the cellar. I could sense the tension in the group. I decided it wasn't safe because I didn't know how the energy would affect everyone. I got up to leave but the lady who sat beside me couldn't move. She lost all sense of feeling from the waist down. The energy from the shadow person had stopped where she was sitting. With no time to waste, I picked her up and carried her up the stone stairs and into the kitchen. That did the trick. Feeling returned and she became calm, in fact so calm she wanted to go back down. Although I did many other visuals in that cellar I never felt the same again. I think once shadow ghosts have been disturbed, they move to another area where they can avoid being noticed.

For the rest of the night I sat in Annabella's room (named after the spirit of a little girl we released back into the spirit world) and did one-on-one mediumship and aura readings. I would start about one in the morning and finishing at 9:00 a.m. The queue would be halfway around the house. It was serous and also a lot of fun. I met Sally during one of these readings. She only came along because her friend wanted to see a ghost. Although interested, she didn't believe either way. Imagine the scene; It's 4:00 a.m. I had set in Annabella's room for three hours with the mediumship readings going well. I still had twenty or so people to see. I had time for a drink of water then onto the next. The door opened and in walked Sally with her warm enchanting smile. With some people you relax. I wasn't expecting anything out of the ordinary so when her grandmother came through by name and told me Sally was wearing her engagement ring; I saw the look in Sally's eyes that I had seen in many before. It was the look of surprise but excitement.

I could hear her thinking, "There really could be something to this mediumship stuff." Then the tears started.

I was shown that Sally had no movement in her right middle finger, "No matter how hard you try it just won't move will it?" I asked.

Holding up her right hand she demonstrated that spirit was right, she had trapped it in a door when young. I could feel the memories of childhood come flooding back, the tears rolled down her cheeks. Then a very young man's voice came into my range. I saw him right in the middle of my mind; tall, blond, muscular with a soft but strong voice.

"Wish Sally luck from me," he said.

Deep breath: "I have a tall blond man in his mid twenty's wishing you luck." I continued, "He would have liked to be with you both on your big day."

Sally's face changed into sadness. She knew this man but didn't want to think he could not be with them both two weeks later when she got married. She looked at me in amazement; I never thought he would be able to come through so soon.

The tall blond man's name was Chris. He was Sally's fiancée and best friend. They served together in the Army's Special Forces up until a month before. Chris was blown up in a bomb attack on his apartment while working undercover in the Middle East. Apparently his death had a terrible effect on them both putting a cloud over the wedding. Chris was to have been the best man. I sat with Sally for well over an hour that night. The message she received was enough to prove beyond doubt she should go ahead with her wedding. Chris would also be with them, even if in spirit. Two weeks later Sally got married and I received wonderful photographs of Sally and her new husband looking very happy together. I knew Chris was right there with them both.

Part of working at Ghosthouse was organizing séances. With most séances nothing much happens. I've never been a believer in moving a glass around a table. It proves nothing. In inviting people to take part I always chose very carefully at Ghosthouse. So for any of you wanting to hold your séance here are a few guide lines for you to consider:

There are three important factors to consider when conducting a séance. They are; the purpose, the quality of the sitters and the location. Each of these must be provided to increase the expectation for a reasonably successful outcome.

The conducting medium:

The medium should be one who has presided over a séance before and is familiar with the importance of insuring that the basic requirements above are met. The séance may be conducted by an inexperienced person; however, the success of the outcome may be affected because of a lack of atonement. In either case, it is up to the conducting medium to assure that the conditions outlined below are also met.

Purpose:

The purpose for the séance should be established prior to the meeting. Is it to contact someone's deceased relative or friend, find spirit guides or to conjure apparitions? Whatever the purpose it must be the only purpose for all the sitters and this must be the only thought in everyone's mind. There cannot be divided purposes in the circle once it begins because it will weaken or destroy the singleness of psychic energy needed in the séance. It is up to the conducting medium to query each sitter and to make them aware of the importance of a single mind among them all. All thoughts of personal affairs, the day's events or any other distracting thoughts must be put aside because these interfere with maintaining a single energy.

The Sitters:

A primary qualification for a sitter is the desire to be there. Without this you lose the expectation that gives the séance that special feeling. If you have to drag someone into the circle, you're doing the wrong thing. Here are the types of people you want in the circle:

Someone who really wants to be there, who is serious and not frivolous, silly and giddy. Positive and uplifting people will add their energy.

A family member who wants to make contact with a deceased loved one. (In the case of seeking such contact) They must not be grasping and groping for the connection but rather subjective and patient for whatever comes. Grasping, desperate persons sometimes block the energy so they must put their feelings in check and be neutral.

Persons who are empathetic and can inject love into the séance. Love is the vibration of communication in the spirit world. Its presence enables communication to take place.

Avoid these people:

The skeptical and cynical person will act like a sinker. Just one will drain the entire circle of its energy and the result will fulfill the skeptic's expectations. Even if it is a family member, do not allow this person to be a part of it.

A fear-filled person has almost the same effect as the skeptic because fear is one of the great negatives that have a counter-effect to the positive love vibration. Their fear may be self-generated or the result of religious superstition. Nevertheless avoid this one also.

Anyone full of hate or envy for anyone in the circle or outside of it will have the same deleterious effect as the previous two.

Location:

There are two best choices. The first is to hold it in a neutral location free from outside disturbances, noises and interference, preferably one that has been previously used for this purpose. Next is to hold it in a place that has a symbolic connection to the purpose. For example, hold it in the home of a deceased person you're trying to establish contact with because there will be objects and artifacts that still have their owner's imprint within them. Incidentally, personal artifacts can also be brought to a neutral meeting place.

The gathering for the séance:

Wait until everyone is present. Then sit around and make small talk for about twenty minutes to give everyone time to settle down and get accustomed to the setting. Then you will be able to begin.

The séance format:

Everyone should sit in a circle, either around a table or with straight back chairs. They should be close enough to hold hands but not touching knees. The lights should be dim or you can use candles. You need just enough light to see everyone's face. Do not conduct the meeting in total darkness as it's not necessary.

Play soft meditative music in the background for at least ten minutes. Then its time for the conducting medium to remind all present that the love vibration carries communication and to invoke it now. Then the purpose is said aloud to everyone. When seeking spirit guides remind everyone to remember any feelings, visions and thoughts they receive in the session so they can be shared with all present. For conjuring apparitions they get the same injunction because most apparitions will be visions they receive when their eyes are closed, not open. When the séance is to invoke a deceased person's spirit the same rules apply except they are told to send the love vibration to the spirit sought and hold the person in loving remembrance.

They should be encouraged not to accept any message or information that has silliness or frivolity associated with it. They should firmly reject it and continue to wait for something more substantial.

Allow twenty to thirty minutes for everyone to stay in this loving remembrance state and then softly request them to return their attention to the circle and open their eyes when ready.

After a few minutes they should all be alert and ready to talk. Start anywhere in the circle and encourage everyone to share their experience. What you are looking for is profound information that has evidence of a connection within it. Look for duplicate messages, visions or feelings which are confirmations of a connection with the spirit.

A recording can be made of the message part of the séance for future reference.

Don't expect a voice from the corner of the room or from within an object. That only happens in the movies. Remember that those in spirit must try just as hard as we do in order to communicate. They are not specialists. They are who they were when they were here in physical bodies. These séances sometimes require repeat sessions to get sufficient details to piece together a coherent picture. Patience is required.

To conjure an apparition, you have to look for the number of similarities in the information of the sitters. Many times there will be a number of people who get the same message or vision or feeling during the session. These are confirmations of a single spirit's influence during the séance.

Follow the above and you will enjoy the experience, you will stay safe, and you might just get that contact that proves there is no such thing as death.

There isn't much in life we know for sure. We search for proof beyond doubt. How many people have received messages from the spirit world in which the medium giving out the information follows up with the phrase "Do you understand?" I think that if people didn't understand they would tell you. The message is for the person not the medium. As a medium I have no reason to doubt the message being given through me.

Red Cloud taught me to give the information and move on. Each contact can give comfort so you should always work hard to reach as many souls as allow. As a young man I watched other mediums work, often by visiting Spiritual Churches across the country. I never went for any reason other than to watch and learn how to work on a platform. I've been lucky enough to watch some of the best mediums this country has offer. I've seen fantastic proof being given out, different personalities doing the same work for the love of it. The best of the best was a little old lady. She was in her late seventies, her body stooped, a walking stick in her left hand, deep blue eyes, her voice gentle but commanding. The church on that winter evening was barely half full; most people were tucked in at home in front of a fire.

They missed an unforgettable evening; one that stays with me many years later every time I stand in front of an audience. I have never seen such a demonstration of proof of spirit given by one person. She started not by standing on the platform but by sitting at the front on a chair. Standing up slowly, her voice changed. She was speaking French to herself, then Chinese then back to English. Walking up and down the aisle, she stopped next to a person, giving a message not waiting for a reply; moving on to the next person, still talking in three languages. She translated the words as if talking to two assistants, her guides. It was a remarkable two hours.

You know when you don't want something to end? That was how I felt. It was spellbinding. By the time she finished everyone in the congregation was given their own personal proof. About thirty-five people sat stunned, in awe of her ability. From that day on that was the level I needed to strive for.

I work very hard to improve the standard of my mediumship. For me, it's not enough to say, "You're only as good as your last message." Red Cloud keeps my feet firmly on the ground with little said when I get things right. My reward is in people's reactions and faces. But I do know that without spirit by my side I'm nothing. I will always take any help offered. Believe me when you're on stage looking out at expectant faces, every one of them waiting for a small sentence, you need help.

I've often asked, "What happens if nothing happens?" I don't tell jokes, sing or dance. This is where my angels help me.

The morning of a stage show about ten years ago, I was doing what I normally did to prepare, (and you thought I just turned up!). Meditation the morning before is necessary. That's when spirit helps me link with the souls of the people who will be in attendance that night. I like to walk on stage and look for the people that stand out. I was just starting to go into my world of meditation. All I could see was orbs of light instead of seeing my tree. They were all swirling around my head, spiraling down getting close then I realized that these weren't orbs. They were winged creatures; hundreds of angels all flying round my head. The colors were literally out of this world. This was my first contact with angels. I had heard of people encountering them, even being helped by them, but I never thought they would come in a swarm. Now my head was spinning. I knew I could take the demonstration of mediumship to a different level tonight. That evening the evidence was amazing. I felt my angels with me, reuniting the two sides of life. It was like they were guiding the souls of the spirit people towards the hall, helping me link then moving onto the next message. I felt fantastic with energy vibrating at a high level; I could have gone on all night. This was the standard I wanted to achieve ever since seeing that lady medium work all those years before. Something else came out of that evening. The next morning I was so taken by the pictures in my mind that I decided it would be good if I could give something back to them in appreciation. But what? How could I help them?

At times like these I do what I normally do, which is, meditate to find the answer. During that meditation the answer was made clear. It was like I was talking to a circle of energy. I had to draw or paint the visions that I saw, sending the pictures to whoever was in need of love anywhere in the world. My task was to make people aware of the energy and love angels could bring to their lives through thought. I was told that I had to complete a million individual pieces of Angel Art. I'm no artist. The last time I had picked up a paintbrush was at school. I was determined though. I had to show others what I was seeing in my mind. The images flowed and the artwork got better and better. Amazingly people liked them! They are now as much a part of my life as Red Cloud. I get requests from all over the world for my angel pictures from many different people for many different reasons. I've been able to raise a lot of money for charity. Not bad for a person who couldn't even draw blood.

Chapter Six

Electric Messages

I always search for the proof of life after passing. My personal knowledge of the soul and its continuing journey isn't always enough. Personal experience of something is a must. At Ghosthouse I allowed people to experience things that they couldn't have imagined in normal life. I set up tape recorders in many rooms hoping to pick up a noise or voice on the magnetic tape. This is known as Electronic Voice Phenomena or EVP for short. This comes under the umbrella of Instrumental Trans Communications (ITC), which includes any electrical appliances from televisions, telephones, computers, and fax machines that spirit can use to make contact with this side of life.

I recorded something of interest once in over fifty attempts. On that occasion the voice on the tape, although slow, couldn't be explained in any rational way. Spirit works in strange ways. I've always know that but the quest to find the answers to this recording lead me into a world that I had no idea existed. To the extent that would unfold before my eyes, here is what I discovered

ITC has a history spanning more than a hundred years. Its initial concept can be traced back to 1901 when American ethnologist, Waldemar Bogoras, visited a shaman of the Tchouktchi tribe in Siberia where he watched a spirit conjuring ritual in a dark room. While putting himself into a trance the shaman beat a drum with increasing rapidity. In bewilderment, Bogoras heard strange voices fill the room coming from all quarters and speaking in both English and Russian.

Afterwards, Bogoras wrote, "I set up my equipment so I could record without light. The shaman sat in the furthest corner of the room, approximately twenty feet away from me. When the light was extinguished the spirits appeared after some 'hesitation.' It followed the wishes of the shaman and spoke into the horn of the phonograph."

On playback of the recording, there was a clear difference between the voice of the shaman, which was audible in the background, and the voices of the "conjured spirits" which appeared to be located at the mouth of the horn. All through the recording, the incessant sound of the shaman's drum could be heard which proved that he had remained stationary. This essentially was the first known EVP or experiment that captured spirit voices using an electrical recording device.

Another official report from 1910 records a Brazilian Catholic altar boy who saw his priest, Father Roberto Landell do Moura talk to a small box that talked back. Because the Catholic Church disapproves of any form of spirit communication other than the traditional concept of prayer the priest would not discuss the box.

The inventor of the electric light, the motion picture camera, and phonograph, Thomas Alva Edison, attempted to build a machine capable of communication with the spirit world in the 1920's.

His assistant, Dr Miller Hutchinson, wrote, "Edison and I are convinced that in the fields of psychic research much will yet be discovered. Facts will prove of greater significance to the thinking of the human race than all the inventions we have ever made in the field of electricity."

Edison is believed to have said that, "If our personality survives, then it is strictly logical or scientific to assume that it retains memory, intellect, other faculties and knowledge that we acquire on this Earth. Therefore, if we can evolve an instrument so delicate as to be affected by our personality as it survives in the next life, such an instrument, when made available, ought to record something."

Edison was a factual scientist and yet upon his deathbed he remarked to his doctor "It is very beautiful over there."

Edison died before his machine was complete but taking into account his nature as a serious scientist, would he have made such a statement unless he believed it to be true?

Telephones have been associated with ITC In his book, *Voices From Beyond By Telephone*, the Brazilian researcher Oscar d'Argonell, reported details of telephone conversations with friends in the spirit world. These conversations include a number of interesting and verifiable explanations of how spirit calls are made.

The American photographer, Attila Von Szalay, experimented with a record cutter. He enjoyed a modicum of success in 1936. He captured spirit voices on phonograph records. He had better success during the 1940's with a wire recorder. Szalay collaborated with the writer Raymond Bayless in the 1950s. The two men documented Von Szalay's results in an article for the American Society for Psychical Research in 1959. Strangely enough, not a single response was received from readers.

In 1949 Marcello Bacci of Grosseto, Italy, began paranormal related experiments. He recorded voices using a vacuum tube radio. A spirit team developed around his work and they spoke to him through the radio. After a period of time, people began visiting his home laboratory to talk to their departed loved ones through Mr. Bacci's radio. Today Marcello Bacci still uses his vacuum tube radio with his spirit friends not only talking to him but singing to him. In the early 1950s in Italy two Catholic priests, Father Ernetti, an internationally respected scientist, physicist, philosopher and music lover and Father Gemelli, a President of the Papal Academy, got together to conduct music research. On

September 15, 1956, Gemelli and Ernetti were recording a Gregorian chant. A wire on their magneto-phone kept breaking. In a moment of exasperation, Father Gemelli asked his father for help. To the amazement of the two men his father's voice, recorded on the magneto-phone, answered him saying, "Of course I shall help you. I'm always with you."

The experiment was repeated and the second experiment produced a very clear voice filled with humor saying, "But Zucchini, it is clear, don't you know it is I?"

Zucchini was a nickname his father gave Father Gemelli. No one knew this nickname his father used to tease him with as a boy. It was obvious that he was truly speaking with his father but despite his joy at this proof of survival, his religious background proved too much for him because of the Catholic Church's belief with regards to spirit communication. This in turn raised the question of his right to speak with the dead. The two men visited Pope Pius XII in Rome where the deeply troubled Father Gemelli explained the experience to the Pope.

Much to Father Gemelli's surprise the Pope reassured him by saying, "Dear Father Gemelli, you really need not worry about this. The existence of this voice is strictly a scientific fact and has nothing whatsoever to do with spiritism. The recorder is totally objective. It receives and records only sound waves from wherever they come. This experiment may perhaps become the cornerstone for a building for scientific studies which will strengthen people's faith in a hereafter."

Despite this reassurance, Father Gemelli made sure that the experiment did not go public until the last years of his life. The results were finally published in 1990.

The great pioneer of the recording of voice phenomena, Swedish film producer Friedrich Juergenson, captured voices on audiotape while recording bird songs in 1959. Playback of the tape revealed a male voice talking about "bird voices in the night."

He listened more closely and heard his mother's voice saying, in German, "Friedrich, you are being watched. Friedel, my little Friedel, can you hear me?"

After hearing his mother's voice, Juergenson was convinced that he had made "an important discovery." Juergenson continued to tape hundreds of spirit voices over the course of the next four years. He, played the tapes at an international press conference and published a book in Swedish in 1964 entitled *Voices from the Universe,* followed by another titled *Radio Contact With The Dead.*

Nineteen sixty seven was a good year for ITC with Franz Seidel of Vienna developing the "psycho-phone." Theodore Rudolph developed a goniometer for Raudive's experiments and Thomas Edison spoke through West German clairvoyant Sigrun Seuterman, in trance. He spoke about his efforts to build a machine for the purposes of recording spirit voices in 1928. Edison also suggested modifying television sets by tuning them to seven hundred forty-megahertz to get paranormal effects. (Session recorded on tape by Paul Affolter, Liestal, Switzerland). Juergenson's *Radio Contact With The Dead,* was translated into German. The Latvian psychologist, Dr Konstantin Raudive, read it with a great deal of skepticism. He visited Juergenson to understand his methodology and decided to experiment on his own. He soon developed his own experimental techniques. As with Juergenson, Raudive also heard the voice of his deceased mother calling him by his boyhood name. "Kostulit, this is your mother." Raudive cataloged thousands of voices under strict laboratory conditions.

Father Leo Schmid conducted EVP experiments in his parish in Oeschgen, Switzerland in 1968. He published his results in a book called *When The Dead Speak,* in 1976 shortly after his death. Also in 1968, Raudive published his book *Unhoerbares wird hoerbar,* (The Inaudible Becomes Audible) based on some seventy two thousand voices he had recorded.

The chief engineers of Pye Records Ltd. conducted a controlled experiment with Konstantin Raudive in 1971. He was invited to their sound laboratory where special equipment was installed to block out any radio and television signals. Raudive was not permitted to touch the equipment. Raudive used one tape recorder, monitored by a control tape recorder. All he was allowed to do was to speak into a microphone. Raudive's voice was taped for eighteen minutes and none of the engineers heard any other sounds. But upon playback of the tape, and much to their amazement, over two hundred voices were heard on it.

Electro-Voice Phenomenon (EVP) experimentation became very popular throughout Europe during the 1960's and 70's. Many individuals and groups collected voices on home tape recorders.

In 1971, Paul Jones, G. W. Meek and Hans Heckman opened a laboratory in America where and undertook the first serious research to create a two-way voice communication system. This was far more sophisticated equipment than that previously used in EVP research.

In 1972, Peter Bander from England wrote *Carry On Talking.* It was published in the United States as *Voices From The Tapes: Recordings from the Other World,* in 1973.

In 1973, Joseph and Michael Lamoreaux of Washington State in the United States had success recording spirit voices after reading Raudive's book. In 1975, Hollywood scriptwriter and playwright, William Addams Welch, wrote *Talks With The Dead.*

A significant breakthrough occurred in the late 1970's. Ironically it was in the United States where EVP had been largely ignored. During 1973, spiritual researchers George and Jeannette Meek met with a gifted medium named William O'Neil. He was both clairvoyant and clairaudient. The Meeks provided funding and direction for a project relating to advanced spirit communication. O'Neil provided the necessary mediumistic and electronics skills.

O'Neil collaborated with several spirit friends on the project including the spirit of Dr George Jeffries Mueller, a deceased university professor and NASA scientist. Mueller appeared as a semi-materialized apparition one day in O'Neil's living room and announced that he would help in the project. It was a most unusual and bizarre collaboration between the two dimensions: Doctor Mueller in spirit helped Bill O'Neil design new electro-magnetic equipment capable of converting spirit voices into audible voices. This equipment became known as the Spiricom. It was a device with tone generators and frequency generators emitting thirteen tones that spanned the range of the adult male voice.

My tape was never explained and all the people I contacted were experts in their fields. They couldn't find a logical reason why the voice left an imprint on the magnetic tape. My view on the paranormal has always been there is nothing paranormal, just some things we can't understand. This was one of those things no one could find the answers to, a paranormal experience.

The autumn of 1980 saw the progress of the Spiricom advance to a point where Doctor Mueller's spirit voice, although still distorted, gained volume and become more defined. Meek and O'Neil had a catalogue of twenty plus hours of communication with their ghostly teammate. For details of these conversations, read George Meek's book, *After We Die, What Then?*

George Meek made a transglobal journey in 1982 distributing tape recordings of sixteen excerpts of dialogues between William J. O'Neil and an American scientist who died fourteen years earlier. He also distributed a one hundred page report giving technical details such as wiring diagrams, photographs, technical specifications and guidelines for continued research by third party groups.

These initial efforts set a worldwide explosion of ideas and theories into place. The American Association of Electronic Voice Phenomenon (AAEVP) was set up in 1982 by Sarah Estep. She compiled a list of many EVP researchers who received her newsletter. She also wrote a popular book called *Voices Of Eternity.* Across Europe, a great many people started to follow the EVP work of researchers such as Friedrich Juergenson and Konstantin Raudive. Naturally there was great excitement and much inspiration from the news of the Spiricom. Reports of telephone calls from the Spirit World became widespread. Many were catalogued by D. Scott Rogo in his 1979 book, *Telephone Calls From The Dead.* Between 1980 and 1981 Manfred Boden of West-Germany obtained unsolicited computer printouts from alleged "spirit" communicators. Prior to that he received telephone calls most often. Up until 1983 he also had unsolicited contacts with communicators of non-human evolution.

Since the advent of the Spiricom the subject of ITC has enjoyed a popular following. Among the many notable names that have come to the fore are Ken Webster of England, Maggy and Jules Harsch-Fischbach of Luxembourg, researchers Klaus Schreiber, Manfred Boden, Hans Otto Koenig, Friedrich Malkhoff, and Adolf Homes all of Germany.

Between 1982 and 1988, Hans Otto Koenig developed a new series of spirit communication technologies that employed extremely low frequency oscillators and lights in the ultraviolet and infrared range. In 1983, Koenig appeared on Radio Luxembourg. Under the close supervision of the station engineers and the host, Rainer Holbe, Koenig set up his equipment.

When one of the engineers asked if it was possible for a voice to come through in a direct reply to a question, a voice replied, "We hear your voice. Otto Koenig makes wireless contact with the dead."

Rainer Holbe was stunned. He had millions of listeners across Europe. "I tell you, dear Listeners of Radio Luxembourg and I swear by the life of my children, that nothing has been manipulated. There are no tricks. It is a voice and we do not know from where it comes."

Ken Webster of the United Kingdom, received around two hundred fifty spirit messages in his computers in the period 1984 to 1985. They came from a Sixteenth Century Englishman named Thomas Harden who apparently "haunted" Webster's house and claimed he had owned the same house four centuries earlier. The spirit of Harden was apparently stuck in time constantly referring to Webster's computer as a "light box."

He typed a message onto the screen on one occasion, "What strange words you are speaking, although I must admit that I had only a poor school education myself. You are a good person and you have a fantastic wife. But you live in my house. It was a big crime to steal my home."

Many of the messages from Harden were written in the Olde English dialect containing some in-depth details of his personal life as well as life in that era. Research at Oxford Library later confirmed many of these facts and Webster's book, *The Vertical Plane,* contains details of those ITC contacts.

In 1985, Klaus Schreiber began receiving spirit images on his television set. They included the faces of scientist Albert Einstein, Austrian actress Romy Schneider and various members of his family including his two dead wives and daughter Karin, with whom he was particularly close. Set up by his colleague, Martin Wenzel, Schreiber's technique was to aim a video camera at the television and feeding the output of the camera back into the television thereby creating a feedback loop. The result was a swirling mist on the screen out of which the spirit faces would slowly form over a succession of frames. In 1985, these amazing results formed the subject of a television documentary and subsequent book by the Radio Luxembourg presenter who interviewed Hans Otto Koenig and Rainer Holbe in nearby Luxembourg.

Again in 1985, a series of spectacular voice contacts through radio systems were obtained by Maggy Harsch-Fischbach and her husband Jules Harsch of Luxembourg in their early experiments. A high-pitched, computer-like voice came through their radios with growing frequency to announce the beginning and end of experiments and to share amazing insights with the couple.

The alleged spirit producing the voice identified itself as an ethereal being who was never human, never animal and never in a physical body. "I am not energy and I am not a light being. You are familiar with the picture of two children walking across a bridge and behind them is a being that protects them. That's what I am to you, but without the wings. You can call me Technician, since that is my role in opening up this communication bridge. I am assigned to Planet Earth."

The couple's small flat became a place of amazing occurrences with visiting scientists and reporters seeing spirit-world images flash across the television screen and hearing long dialogues by numerous deceased personalities through radio.

The spirit of Nelson D. Rockefeller told German physicist Ernst Senkowski, "The Mahatmas are a reality."

Nineteenth Century chemist Henri Ste. Claire de Ville told a group of international researchers, "It is our job as well as your job to set fire to minds. To set fire to minds in your world and in that moment to try to master time." In 1994, the spirit of Konstantin Raudive stated, in English, through the radios, "It can only work when the vibrations of those present are in complete harmony and when their aims and intentions are pure." He went on to address those present, person by person, with a personal message for each of them.

Fritz Malkhoff and Adolf Homes independently began ITC experiments in 1987; both rapidly captured spirit voices on tape. After a number of months, they learned of each other's work and became colleagues and friends. Small voices on radio quickly developed long, clear voices during their experiments. They began to receive phone calls from spirit friends and in 1988, they set up Malakoff's computer in the house of Adolf Homes where they did the majority of their experiments. They posed a short question and two days later a short reply appeared on the computer screen. Malkhoff received many phone calls from spirit friends as the years went by including some from "nature spirits." Homes routinely received spirit images on his television and messages on his computer screen. Homes climbed out of bed one morning in 1994, in a trance he aimed a video camera at the television and received the first color picture from the Spirit World. It was an image of deceased EVP pioneer, Friedrich Juergenson.

As this happened, Homes' computer printed out a message from Juergenson stating, "This is Friedel from Sweden. I am sending you a self-portrait. The projection since January 17, 1991 has been in the quantum of spacelessness and timelessness. All your thoughts have their own electromagnetic reality, which does not get lost outside the space-time structure. Consciousness creates all form."

ITC entered a new phase of development in 1995. Mark Macy, working closely with ITC colleagues on both sides of the Atlantic, planned a meeting among scientists and researchers from different countries. A group of sixteen people met in England to discuss this new concept, what potential it had for the world, and what obstacles existed that would impede further envelopment. New friendships were formed and by the end of a long weekend INIT, the International Network for Instrumental Trans-communication, came into being. During the ensuing months, ethereal beings stated they were closely observing this group's efforts and would provide guidance and support. The group began to experience unprecedented advances and events in their research. Many of them received phone calls, usually from the spirit of Konstantin Raudive and the Harsch-Fischbachs received amazing pictures and messages through their computer. This was all a result of the resonance between the INIT members. The evidence was clear that a new era of ITC research had begun. The ethereal beings told the group that the greatest strides would be made by individuals from different countries who committed to work together in harmony with pure intentions.

The aging pioneers were dying. Konstantin Raudive passed away in 1974, Friedrich Juergenson in 1987, Klaus Schreiber in 1988, Bill O'Neil in 1991 and George Meek in 1999. But as they died, they began to get in touch with their colleagues on Earth through ITC systems. Raudive told several colleagues that since his death it had been his calling to continue the development of ITC systems from the spirit side. He called Macy on the telephone seven times after his death. On one occasion they chatted for nearly fifteen minutes before the contact ended. On another occasion he told Macy to purchase a "VLF converter" for his radio system, as it would improve the quality of the contacts. Friedrich Juergenson told watching ITC researchers in Germany, through the television of Adolf Homes, "Every being is a unity of spirit and body that cannot be separated on earth or in spirit. The only difference is the fact that the physical body disintegrates and in its place comes the astral body. Our message is to tell you that your life goes on. Any speculations on how an individual will experience it are bound to be limited in accuracy. All your scientific, medical, or biological speculations miss the mark of these realities. What serves as 'real' to science is not close to reality in the broad picture. It is no more than a word in a book."

The most inspiring and useful information that came through to the group was from a number of timeless beings who said they had never been in physical bodies but had observed human development over many thousands of years. These ethereal beings addressed the group in 1996, stating, "This is the seventh time that we accompany and guide you on your progress toward a free, wealthy and sane future in which humanity will strip off the chains of intolerance and cruelty—a future in which it will be able to establish a fruitful, endurable relationship with the light, ethereal realms of existence."

On more than one occasion, beings from the ethereal world told members of INIT that simply opening the door to the Spirit World could be dangerous. But researchers who worked together and dedicated their efforts to higher human principles would receive ethereal guidance and protection. As the years passed, Technician and his six ethereal friends, along with a

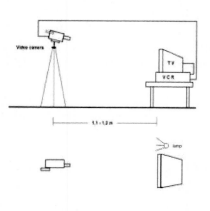

97

team of more than one thousand spirit beings who had once lived on Earth, shared vast and astonishing information with the INIT members through computers, telephones, radios and other technical media. The ethereal beings said they had accompanied this world for many thousands of years and had come close six times when the Earth had reached a crossroads leading either to a dark age or to a period of enlightenment. This, they said, was the seventh time and they wished to establish a lasting bridge between Earth and their formless realm of wise, loving consciousness. ITC research would be the means by which to establish that bridge and through the work of INIT it became evident that the more miraculous forms of ITC contacts were made possible by such ethereal beings who provided protection and guidance for ITC researchers and their spirit colleagues.

The ethereal beings told the INIT members that the collective wisdom and knowledge of all the INIT members allowed the information in ITC contacts to contain an unprecedented depth of substance. Thanks to a collective understanding, they were told about the distant past of the world, long before recorded history, and were given hints about a number of future possibilities depending on the critical decisions of humans in the near future. The ethereal beings also told of what it's like, from their perspective, when they come to "take us home" at the end of an earthly life.

These are just a few general examples of the types of information delivered through ITC systems: ITC contacts are made possible by a contact field, which is a pool of thoughts and attitudes of all researchers collaborating on an ITC project, as well as the thoughts and attitudes of their spirit team. When the thoughts and attitudes of all the entities on both sides of the veil are in harmony, the spirit friends told them that the contact field was clear. They could then see into this world and work with the team's equipment. When doubts, fears, envy, resentment and other troubled feelings created dissonance, the contact field became cloudy, and the spirit friends said that they could not see easily into this world or work with the equipment.

That's what happened to INIT. Troubles began to develop after several years. Many of the group became insecure about the amazing contacts they were receiving. Effectively, they had no way of understanding what it was that was making them possible. In due course, many of them believed that they would not make the major strides in ITC research until science became involved and discovered the secrets behind ITC contacts. Some members began working with scientists in their home country, who, when looking at the results of the research, told the INIT researchers that the miracles they had been receiving were scientifically impossible. The scientists told the INIT members that they should be more skeptical of the contacts being reported. Some members began to publicly express doubts about the legitimacy of other member's contacts. This created a feeling of betrayal among the receiving researchers and a division was created within the association. Some felt that INIT should work alongside science even if it did mean taking a more skeptical approach. Others believed that the astounding contacts were of the great importance and those scientists who were not ready, willing, or able to accept the legitimacy of the group's work should be forgotten. Fueled by conflict, animosity and bruised feelings, the division rapidly grew on both sides of the Atlantic and possibly on both sides of the veil as well.

The result of this was dissonance. The contact field became cloudy, the ethereal beings were unable to come through and work with the INIT equipment and the amazing results of ITC virtually dried up. To date, there have been no phone calls, Faxes, detailed computer images and texts from the Spirit World with messages of great depth and import reported from any researchers since the year 2000.

There is a belief that those miracles and many more will return when man has learned from his mistakes, when man realizes that the doubts, fears, insecurities, envy, resentment, and the other dark feelings which humans experience on a day to day basis. This is taken for granted as a part of life while on Earth and must be kept under control when involved in any form of spiritual work, particularly ITC research. It is a very easy thing to say that we are in harmony with others. But hidden doubts, fears, and insecurities dictate otherwise. Those dark feelings inside must be found and brought into the light so that they can heal.

Humans are spirit magnets, attracting spiritual influences that resonate with our attitudes. If there is doubt or fear, this will attract spirits who will stir up doubts and fears. If there is an encompassing love and trust, this will attract spirits who will support that love and trust.

Future ITC networks that will enjoy miracles in the future are those that grow upon a foundation of harmony. As has been said previously, the ethereal beings told the INIT members on several occasions that opening door to the Spirit World could be dangerous, working together and dedicating efforts to higher human principles will receive guidance and protection.

Chapter Seven

The Falklands

Being a medium myself I rarely went for a private sitting. Why should I ask others to give me a reading when I could talk with spirit? Sometimes it's nice to hear it from others. It stops me from thinking that I'm going slightly mad.

When I parked my car outside a large Victorian house, the street lined with trees, bright green in their splendor, I wasn't sure why I was drawn to this person's front door. The door opened into a dark hall way, a small middle aged woman, with a round face, red hair and broad smile on her face said, "Come in young man, I've been expecting you." I was shown into a small side room, pictures of angels hung from the walls and crystals were scattered randomly among the shelves of books and figurines.

I sat down and wasn't surprised when my father came through. He had died four years earlier but since his passing I had become close to him He was always somewhere in the background.

"He's so proud of you," she started.

I nodded. I knew he was pleased that the year before I had followed his steps and joined the Royal Air Force. He always wanted me to have a chance for a career in the Air Force when

I was younger. Of course I had rejected this out of hand not being one for discipline. Now at the age of twenty-two I finally gave in and signed up. You could say that I took the long way around. It was nice to hear a stranger that I never met tell me things I already knew!

Then without any warning the lady said to me "You're going down the Falklands. Your dad has just shown me a penguin."

Now this was the first I had heard of this. The war in the Falklands had just finished. It was the last place in the world I wanted to go. She went on, "You're not to worry. George and Katie will be coming too!"

That sealed it I was going.

"No harm will come to you." Now I knew why I had come to see this lady; it was spirit's way of preparing me for another lesson.

"You will even find a fish and chip shop!"

I felt the warmth in her voice as she continued to relay messages. I made a mental note of every word, knowing the experience would change my life. Through personal choice, one of these situations would lead to a better understanding of what it would be like to face death. I wasn't in the least bothered about the personal risk of being in a war zone. In fact I was excited at the prospect of seeing the landmarks that were front-page news a year ago at first hand.

Later that year, the prophecy became reality. I was to fly down to the Falkland Isles after the Christmas holidays; I would spend one hundred twenty six days there, returning home early June. This meant I would be on the Islands during the first anniversary of the conflict.

It was a cold sunny winter morning. The trees were bare and the ground white with frost as I set out on the journey to the airport. The next four and a half months would be an experience that money couldn't buy. But as the car drove to the airport, all I could think of was the message from that medium six months before, "No harm will come to you." I couldn't help but wonder who I would meet and what lay in store eight thousand miles away in the South Atlantic.

The flight was long with a stop on Ascension Isle. By the time we reached the Falklands we had been in the air for over ten hours. As we circled round East Falkland I remember thinking what a forsaken place. No trees, just rocks, moss, and water. Who would even want to live here let alone fight for the privilege? My first reactions were wrong. Again spirit had a way of teaching me lessons in spite of my hasty judgment.

The plane came to a stop. This was it; my home for the next few weeks. RAF airports aren't like Heathrow or Gatwick. Port Stanley airport is very basic; military police, RAF regiment in charge, no messing with them or worrying where your bags were. They were there in the middle of the floor in a giant heap. Find your own if you were brave enough to wade in.

I had just about found my feet and my luggage when I got a tap on my shoulder. I had just flown a quarter way around the world to a land and people I had no prior knowledge of and standing right next to me was my old friend from the county hockey team from back home. I couldn't believe my eyes. Could it really be Kevin? We had been comrades in arms over many battles on the hockey pitch but I never expected to see him grinning like a Cheshire cat in the middle of Port Stanley airport. After the war Kevin had returned to his home on the Falklands. His grandparents were born there so he thought it would be good to have the family back together. So as I was joining up, Kevin was heading home. He had seen my name on the arrivals list and knew it was me. He couldn't wait to introduce me to his family at Goose Green plus he had a few other surprises for me.

At that time the Falklands were a very dangerous place to be not just because of the threat from Argentina, only an hour's flight away, but also from all the land mines that Argentine troops had indiscriminately dropped from helicopters. The whole island was covered in mine fields. It was surreal to see all the barbed wire and red Beware Mines signs. One of the funniest things I saw during my time on the island was a colony of penguins setting in a minefield. They were safe from everything and everyone. The mines were designed to explode when the weight of a man stood on them. The penguins didn't weigh enough. This made it a very safe area for them to nest and bring up their young. I couldn't help but think how ingenious wild life is.

I soon settled down. I worked long hours and my days went fast. Kevin invited me to his farm on my first day off some two weeks later. Transport wasn't easy to come by. It was mainly helicopters, flying supplies and people around the two main islands West and East Falklands. In between was a long stretch of water known as Falkland Sound. For me to get to Goose Green, about fifty miles from Port Stanley, I needed to talk to the helicopter pilots. I was in luck. It seemed most days they flew over to the small farming community. I could fly over one day then back to Stanley the next. This meant I could have a whole day with Kevin.

"You don't do things by half." said a grinning Kevin as I stepped off the army helicopter. The journey over was a new experience for me. It was fantastic flying just above the rugged terrain; the pilots always flew as low as possible. It was like being in a fast car without the bumps as we shot across the granite gray rocks and pools of water. With a wave of gratitude to the crew, I watched the noisy flying machine lurch forward, nose first then disappear over the horizon. So this was Goose Green. It was still battle-scarred where the Argentinean soldiers had dug in to defend it from Two Para. The foxholes were still connected by green communication cable. Kevin told me this was part of their downfall. The Argentines were well positioned, hidden from sight, and all except for the green cable. Two Para followed the cable from foxhole to foxhole. I didn't like the thought that people had spent their last moments in these holes but it was war.

The farmhouse was warm and welcoming; the whole family was there to greet me. I had met his parents on many occasions. They were friendly people with much to share. I was keen to hear a first hand account of what it was like to live through the occupation. But first Kevin wanted to show me around the farm and introduce me to horses, his pride and joys. In back of a few ramshackle buildings was an odd shaped stable. It had stonewalls with a corrugated iron roof. From the outside it looked tiny but when inside seemed far bigger. Looking straight at me were two white and brown horses. I love animals, always have. I could sense their unease as a stranger walked into their home.

So I walked up to the biggest one while saying in my mind "you're beautiful." The mare relaxed allowing me to stroke her head.

Kevin's jaw dropped, "How did you do that?" "Briny never lets anyone other than me anywhere near!"

Since I was a child I have got on well with animals. I believe it's because I show no fear and animals know that. These horses were lovely, a brilliant surprise. Nutmeg, the other horse was also keen to get to know me. I could have spent the rest of the day sitting with them both. Kevin told me he rode Briny up and down the rocky fields. Nutmeg hadn't been broken in long but I was welcome to try. I had only sat on a horse once. When I was only four or five I sat on a large gray mare at the seaside. I could remember how far up it was and being frightened to move once on board.

But this was different, "I would love too," I said.

At that point Kevin broke the news. Every year the population on the Falklands got together and raced their horses against one another. This year's event was planned for early May and I could ride for Goose Green if I wanted to. Now there's a challenge. I had eight weeks to become a competent rider. Nutmeg would be my horse. Over the next few weeks I spent my spare time at Goose Green with my friend Nutmeg, or should I say Kevin!

The weather on the Falklands was the worst you could imagine. The wind would whistle across the island blowing you off your feet. The soil is peat and when wet it can be impossible to walk over. It's bog-like when wet and like fine sand when dry. If you had to walk a long distance, the wind was always blowing and there were no trees to break the wind anywhere, you had a tough walk. I thought to myself that no tree had a chance! It was like being hit by a sand blaster. The winter months run from the end of May through December. The nights are long so during these months the Falkland Islanders have to fit a lot in the little daylight. The two biggest industries are farming, mainly sheep, and fishing for the squid that swim around the shores. The squid are why the penguins set up home in the islands. They attract fishing fleets from all over the world. Life is tough and you must be fit and strong to survive the climate. If the conflict had gone into the Falklands winter I'm sure many more lives would have been lost.

My time at Goose Green was well spent. I looked forward to riding Nutmeg. Everything would be fine; we made a good team. The races were only a few weeks away. I was lucky in that the Falklands Festival was only for the people who had grown up on the Island. I was one of the first outsiders to be invited even though I never felt like an outsider.

During my time at the farm, I wanted to learn a little more of the history of the Falklands. Kevin's dad, Bill explained that before the Argentineans invaded they lived hand-in-hand with their neighbors. Trade links were very good and they were encouraged to date Argentinean women. There were far more single men than women on the Falklands so it made sense that future islanders would be half British, half Argentine. This would have solved the dispute between their governments as joint sovereignty was only years away.

That all changed on the April 2, 1982. The Argentineans took control of the Islands for seventy-two days before surrendering. Bill talked about the Argentines. At first they were courteous. Over one thousand Argentine troops had occupied Goose Green because it had its own airfield. When the British bombed it killing many of the air crew and destroying many Argentinean planes, the mood changed. All the civilians were taken from their homes and put under guard in the social club; one hundred fourteen men, women, and children; the youngest child was only four months old. Conditions were very bad with only two toilets, no beds, and a diet of crackers, spam, and cold baked beans. Bill told me he never wanted to see another baked bean as long as he lived.

After being imprisoned four weeks in the social club, the sound of the British troops approaching was frightening. They feared the building would be hit by a stray shell so they ripped up the floorboards and hid in the foundations. When the Argentine soldiers surrendered, it was with much relief. Welcoming the men with the purple berries was as much about getting away from the prison as it was joy at watching the Argentines hand over their weapons.

However the joy was short-lived. As the residents of Goose Green returned to their houses they found an awful mess; the Argentine troops had lived like animals, with little respect for the homes that they had commandeered. On the door step of one home was the nose cone of a Harrier Jump Jet that was shot down. The pilot, Flight Lieutenant Nicolas Taylor, was killed. The Argentine solders had inscribed the date and time of his death on the nosepiece in triumph. Not a nice thing to find on your door step.

When Two Para won the battle for Goose Green it was the end of one battle and beginning of another. The loss of life on both sides left a deep sorrow in the small community. The Argentine Cemetery was where all the young men who fought to the end were located at Goose Green. It was an isolated spot with simple wooden crosses surrounded by a white wooden fence.

Bill took me there so I could appreciate the sadness. In the wind-blown dull green and gray landscape and overcast sky; all I could think of was the memory of all those lost souls. I had to see if I could pick up on the energy left behind in the atmosphere.

After talking it through with Kevin and his father we came to the conclusion that we should hold a séance. The thinking behind this was if any souls were still earth bound, trapped not knowing what had happened, I could help them move over. It was like I had been drawn to this place for that purpose. Spirit was teaching me so much about death; that it wasn't the end, just the beginning. Here I was many miles from my home, feeling the sadness of many who had lost fathers, husbands, and brothers in another pointless war. Both sides lost.

Having set in motion the thought of a séance, it seemed a good idea to do it as soon as possible. My time was also running out. I only had another six weeks before returning home. I worked it so my time off came all at once towards the end of my tour. Not only did it give me something to look forward to; it also meant that I could spend a whole week with Kevin and his family. I was one of the lucky ones. There wasn't that much to do with any time off. Port Stanley had the Globe Inn and a fish and chip shop which was the best fish and chips you ever tasted. Fresh hocki in batter, very different from the cod we get back home. The Globe was a pub with one difference. It only sold cases of beer; twenty-four cans for around £5. It wasn't hard to see why some spent their off duty time drinking.

During that week, I had three things planned. One was the séance; the second was the festival; and the third was a trip to Mount Tumbledown just outside Stanley.

It felt strange standing in the middle of Goose Green one year after the war. I could almost smell the cordite. The air was heavy with the early morning mist; this is how it would have been the morning after the battle. Most combat took place at night. Today was the day I would try to establish contact. The farmhouse was always warm, like a log cabin made out of stone and corrugated iron. The wind whistled though the roof and you could hear the sound of the flag on top of the poll flapping. For the séance I needed four people; one at each corner of the square wooden table. I laid out the twenty-six letters of the alphabet, a card with YES and a card with NO and 0 to 9 in a large circle. I placed a small glass in the center of the circle. This was all I needed. I said a prayer of protection, cleared my thoughts. Then in turn; Bill, Kevin, Kevin's mum

Mary and I placed our forefingers on the glass resting, on the bottom of the upturned glass.

I began, "IF ANYONE WOULD LIKE TO COME THROUGH PLEASE USE OUR ENERGY."

Nothing. We sat in silence; nothing moved. All I could hear was the flag snapping in the wind.

I tried again, "IF ANYONE WOULD LIKE TO MAKE CONTACT PLEASE USE OUR ENERGY."

Again nothing. Perhaps I was wrong. Maybe there were no spirits.

One last time now really consumed I told myself. "WE ARE HERE FOR YOU PLEASE USE MY ENERGY."

The glass started moving very slow at first, then a little faster, but all it was doing was going round in circles. "PLEASE USE THE GLASS TO INDICATE WHO YOU ARE." The glass stopped almost at once.

"PLEASE USE THE LETTERS AND NUMBERS TO TELL US WHO YOU ARE."

Nothing. The room had a prickly energy, I had felt before. I knew if we could just push a little harder we could make a breakthrough. I could see Kevin, Bill, and Mary all had their eyes closed almost like they didn't want to look, just in case something did happen.

I knew this feeling, "PLEASE IF YOU WOULD LIKE US TO TAKE A MESSAGE FOR YOU USE OUR ENERGY."

The glass started spinning in very small circles, almost like it was trying to pick up enough speed to direct it in the right direction, then very, very slowly it started to move towards the numbers, 2, then back into the center; then across the table P, back again A, faster now R, back into the center then back to the A.

It spelled 2 PARA. THANK YOU. YOU WANT TO TELL US YOU WERE IN 2 PARA?

The glass stops, then moved fast to the YES card.

"CAN YOU TELL US YOUR NAME AND RANK?" Now the glass was moving C. A. P. T. A. I. N. "YOUR RANK WAS CAPTAIN, YES OR NO?"

The glass swung again this time in a loop. YES. "PLEASE TELL US YOUR NAME." D. E. N. T. "YOUR NAME IS CAPTAIN DENT. YOU WERE A MEMBER OF TWO PARA, IS THIS RIGHT?"

The glass now stuck to the table. The others had their eyes wide open watching in amazement. It shot across to the YES. We had a man who claimed to be a Captain Dent from 2 Para.

"CAN YOU GIVE US YOUR FIRST NAME PLEASE?" C. H. R. I. S. "THANK YOU."

The energy was still very static. I went on "DID YOUR LIFE END AT GOOSE GREEN?"

The glass moved straight to the YES card.

"HOW DID YOU FIND YOURSELF IN SPIRIT?" Two words were spelled out. S. H. O. T. and R. A. D. I. O. (At the time I had no idea what the message radio was about. All was to become clear when we researched Captain Dents story.)

The energy was now getting low. I could see the others were getting tried. The séance had lasted over two hours; time to thank The Captain for making contact, say a closing prayer for protection and write up the notes I took during the séance.

I looked across the table to see three very exhausted people. They had never experienced anything like this before (its hard work keeping your arm in one place for two hours... I could see they had reach their limits).

This is the first time I've told this story and it's some twenty-four years after it happened.

This is what I found out after about the circumstances of Captain Chris Dent of Two Para.

In the early hours of May 28, Captain Dent and three companies of 2nd Battalion, The Parachute Regiment, took part in what was to become one of the most famous battles of the campaign. Led by Colonel "H" Jones, the men attacked enemy trenches surrounding the Goose Green settlement. At Colonel Jones's request, Captain Dent braved enemy fire to retrieve a vital radio from a soldier who was killed. The colonel and his men came under renewed fire, their attack threatened to grind to a halt and they were forced to take cover. Captain Dent was warned by a colleague that if he tried to proceed, he would be killed. However, he realized that if the momentum was lost, the lives of his men would be in greater danger and the battle might be lost.

He stood up and sprinted towards the Argentine positions but was cut down by machine-gun fire. Moments later, Colonel Jones, who was posthumously awarded the Victoria Cross for his bravery, was killed as he stormed an enemy trench. The British won the battle but the cost was seventeen men.

Captain Dent was a very brave solider. That he came through to us that morning tells me that his soul carried on after his life was taken. Séances should always be held with the utmost respect.

The whole experience had a deep effect on Kevin and his family, something that he would never forget. A few days later I experienced something new to me; racing a horse against ten others bare back; not for the faint hearted. The experience ended my horse racing for life!

If I ever had aspirations to become a jockey this was the day. The Falklands Festival had arrived. People from all over the island came to celebrate the Independence of the Falklands and to compete against each other in a number of events. The main event was the bareback horse race. I had prepared for this over the last eight weeks with Nutmeg. The racecourse, if you could call it that, was a tight twelve-furlong circle marked out by stakes and orange tape. The ground was soft but unlike some of the terrain, there were no rocks. This was for good reason I learned later that day. All races were twice round the track with first past the post as the winner. There were no rules; it was everyman for himself when the flag dropped. I watched in awe as the first two races took place. It was like watching circus riders hanging on for dear life, circling the ring. A thick track of mud soon formed around the course as the hoofs cut up the soft ground.

Now it was my turn. I had put a lot of hard work in for this moment; I knew how to dig my heels into Nutmeg to get her to go and had taught her that if I pulled the reins towards me she would stop. With this in mind about; all I had to do was hang on! My stomach was jumping as I lined up at the start. Nutmeg was nervous; I could feel her unease but since I was nervous too, perhaps she felt my tension. The white flag dropped, Nutmeg reared and threw me to the ground. I landed in a heap of mud and horse poo and Nutmeg flew around the course riderless. I'm sure she thought she had a better chance of winning without me on her back! Although unhurt, my pride was damaged. I got up from out of the mud looking like the creature from the swamp! I promised myself I would never ride a horse again.

The rest of the festival was very enjoyable. I learned about the culture, the people, and why it was so important for them to remain British. Even before the war, ninety percent of the population, when asked, voted to remain British. That night I had one final treat. Listening to the radio live from Port Stanley! The local radio station would broadcast almost anything. In this case it was darts! And these were pub players who couldn't hit a barn door!

My memories of Goose Green are mixed; being so close to the people that lived through that time was a privilege for me.

I had one last thing to do before returning home and that was to visit Mount Tumbledown. It was nothing like I expected. After reading about how the Scots Guards had taken the highest point overlooking Port Stanley, I felt very humble standing just off the rubble track about one hundred yards away. I could see an artillery gun that was blown up and left in the field in front of the mount. Scattered across the ground were abandoned white blankets-no longer needed. The ground was very rocky, wet, and slippery. Walking to the foot of Mount Tumbledown only took a few minutes. Mount Tumbledown itself looked down. I walked across the field in front then climbed up the rocks to the summit. It took me fifteen minutes. On the night of the battle the Scot Guards took over eighteen hours to do the same! The Argentine soldiers were well dug in six weeks before. They knew that it was a very important location; if Mount Tumbledown fell into British hands the war would be over. The courage of the soldiers on both sides was remarkable. As I climbed to the top to pay my respects next to the wooden and brass cross laid at the summit were the names of the Guardsmen that lost their personal battles I couldn't stop myself thinking what happened that night. Below and stretched out in front of me was Port Stanley harbor. The old wooden cutter ship, abandoned long ago, sat like a guard just off shore, the old-fashioned town glinted in the sunlight. This would have been the view the first Scots Guardsmen would have had of Port Stanley the morning after the battle as they watched the Argentines run down the slope to the town below.

As I started down from the summit, I noticed around back out of sight was a large cooker. It was placed there to feed the Argentinean troops. How it got there was anyone's guess, but there it was and probably still is. This was too good an opportunity to let pass. Psychometry (the art of holding or touching objects to feel the thoughts and history imprinted in the object) has always interested me. I've found that large objects soak up the psychical energy of people around them. Doors are especially good in houses as so many people touch them. So this cooker was a small treasure, having been the central focus point for the men while waiting for the British to attack. I placed my hands on the oven door, closed down my thoughts and relaxed. Visions came flooding in, men laughing and singing, the smell of burning wood, also chaos, like being in the middle of a large crowd of people all wanting to get somewhere fast. I could sense cigarette smoke, then the visions changed, the energy was more focused; bright lights greens, reds, lit up the dark sky. Then nothing but peace. I felt the wind blowing through my hair and was back looking at the cooker. I felt disoriented. The whole experience was far more than I had hoped for. I had just been given a small glimpse into the past.

The last part of my journey was to follow the route the Scots Guards took into Port Stanley the morning after the battle. A twenty minute walk with the strong wind behind me; going down across the field, past the hospital and Government house onto the central road that went through the middle of the town. The large wooden Catholic church stood out, a symbol of peace in this peaceful and un-war like town. I always thought it rather funny that a lot of the buildings were made from timber yet no trees ever grew on the Falklands. Where had all the wood come from?

My memories of the Falklands will always be fond ones. Such as Port Stanley with its narrow little streets quaint houses and no traffic lights. The best fish and chip shop this side of the Atlantic! Darts on the radio, bareback horse racing at Goose Green. The men who will never return home. I changed my mind on my first impressions; it wasn't a forsaken place. It was one of the most beautiful islands you could come across. The people were kind, caring, and proud to be British. I'm sure I left a little piece of myself behind. One day I hope to return to reclaim the friendships I made.

The journey home seemed twice as long as the journey down. I had been away from home for nearly five months. In that time I hadn't seen a tree, read a newspaper, drank fresh milk, or watched television.

At last the plane touched down; my heart jumped at the excitement of seeing family and friends again. The Falkland Islands always seemed very dull, like watching television in black and white. Stepping off the plane the colors were so bright; green grass, blue summer sky and a light breeze not the howling gales that I had become accustomed to. Life was good. I had learned many new lessons. In my mind I thanked spirit knowing I had the next six summer weeks off.

I dedicate this chapter to the men and women who gave so much to allow the Falkland Islanders to decide their own future. And those in the armed forces that still serve keeping the Falklands safe.

Chapter Eight

Protection

My life had moved on in many ways. I was married and a father to two young children with another one on the way. I left the Air Force the year before to settle down in one place. The service life is great while single, moving round every few months, but once the family started to come along it was important to put roots down. I applied to join the Prison Service, was accepted and I was working in a local prison. Again I'm sure spirit had a hand in placing me in a job where I would meet so many different people from all walks of life. The job was extremely challenging. Looking back there was so much negative energy not only from the inmates but also from the staff. Most were good men and women doing a well-paid job they could not afford to give up. They were as trapped as the prisoners they guarded. I watched the older officers going through the motions, counting their days until they could draw their pensions. It was like their souls had been taken; cold cynical, untrusting of one and all and only looking out for themselves. I looked at them knowing I would never want to become dead inside.

To understand prison life is one thing; the routine, everything happened on the same time each day without fail but the smell is something else. Sweat, muck, and bleach all mixed up in one overwhelming stench. I remember feeling sick on my first day and I unlocked the door and gate with the large black keys that hung from my belt. Nothing prepared me for walking into the prison. The building was built over a hundred years ago, and from what I could see, nothing much had changed during that time. It the same as it had always been with different faces occupying the cells and landings. In four stories with up to sixty inmates per landing, around two hundred forty prisoners, all having to be unlocked, fed, taken to work, (jobs included working in the kitchen, laundry, print shop), every inmate had to work. In return they earned £10 per week plus any benefits a job in the kitchen or print shop might provide.

I found out early on that it was a dog-eat-dog environment. The older prison officers put themselves in for the easier duties like working in the gatehouse. This was at the front of the prison; opening the large wooden gates so the transport could come in and out, bringing and taking prisoners to and from the local courts. This duty involved little confrontation unlike working on the landings, which were always a battle. Not only could you find yourself in the middle of a fight or trying to sort out a domestic situation (many inmates get "Dear John" letters while serving time), you also found yourself on the serving line. You looked after the "line" as it was known. This was the area the officers liked least. Inmates get three hot meals a day whether they need them or not; porridge, bacon, sausage, toast, boiled eggs, cereal for breakfast. Lunch consisted of hot pies, pasties, peas, mash potatoes or chips and fish and chips on Friday. Evening meal would be curry, stews, liver, chili, sponge, and custard, with a supper bun or fresh fruit. You also had to serve special diets; vegetarians, religious and vegan. I learned that ninety percent of the country's vegan's were in prison. This was because their food was cooked specially for them; they got soymilk, nuts, and raisins. No wonder the prison population was so high. They got better food than at home. Young officers got the job of keeping order during food service. This was an impossible task. The kitchen inmates stood behind the counter and gave out the different diets. Members of the kitchen staff would hand out the main courses, fruit, and cake. It was chaos. Inmates would try to steal food, intimidate other inmates into giving them more and there was just enough food to go around. If you ran out it was difficult to feed the last landing. I stood on the same side of the counter as the inmates. If trouble occurred, I had a red panic button just above my left shoulder should I need assistance.

I knew this was spirits way of testing me. If I could cope with two hundred sixty inmates, all wanting more than was offered, I would have no problem standing on stage delivering spirit messages to a hall full of expectant folks. Now that I have done both I can tell you I have never felt nervous in front of an audience. There were many times when I knew standing on the line there would be trouble. Big trouble.

The food was handed out on strong metal trays with three compartments; one for each course. If the food was below standard, which it often was, it was common for someone to wear the tray with the food still on it. Being hit by one of those metal trays was no joke especially if it had curry or hot custard. I learned to duck very fast. Others weren't so lucky.

One officer had worked in the prison for a few months. He felt the same way as I did. He watched the senior officers get the soft duties. We laughed about it together and soon formed a good friendship. Tony was in the Navy during the Falklands conflict and had escaped death on several occasions. He decided to leave his life at sea behind for a more settled life in the Prison Service. Tony had served on HMS Sheffield; one of the ships that was attacked in Falkland Sound. He lost several close friends; this was something he was finding hard to come to terms with. He would ask why them and not me? Because of my beliefs we sat and chatted about the afterlife. Was there something more when we die? We had much in common. I saw how depressed he was becoming; his aura grew duller by the day. I knew the job was getting him down. Dealing with demanding people isn't easy when you are at ease with the world. When you felt down everything came down on you. It was easy to slip into depression. So I wasn't surprised when he didn't turn up for work one afternoon. We worked shifts together on a four-week turnaround, from early days to late nights. This week we were starting back on a week of lates: 4 p.m. in the afternoon to 10:30 p.m. Our job was to feed the whole wing, then lock them up for the night. When I came to work the next day I was called into Governor's Office.

His face was long, his voice low, "I have some bad news for you." I didn't relate it to Tony. He said, " Tony is dead."

I was in shock. Although I knew he was going through a tough time, he seemed to be coming out the other end just fine. He was his normal self a few days earlier.

He gassed himself in his car. I felt guilty. I should have been able to help him but couldn't. He made his mind up to end his life. The pressure of work, home and his lost friends had become too much. It was the only way out for him. That's why he was keeping to himself the last few shifts I worked with him. He knew he was going to die, so life became easy; no pressure or worries, just an open door to find his friends in spirit.

Two weeks later I read the eulogy at his funeral. I choose my favorite poet Ella Wheeler Wilcox to say the words I couldn't find.

The Depths
By Ella Wheeler Wilcox

Not only sun-kissed heights are fair below,
The cold, dark billows of the frowning deep,
Do lovely blossoms of the ocean sleep?
Rocked gently by the waters to and fro,
The coral beds with magic colors glow,
And priceless pearl-encrusted mollusks heap,
The glittering rocks where shining atoms leap,
Like living broken rainbows.
Even so,

We find the sea of sorrow black as night,
The sullen surface meets our frightened gaze.
As down we sink to darkness and despair.
But at the depths! Such beauty, such delight!
Such flowers as never grew in pleasure's ways.
Ah! Not alone are sun-kissed summits fair.

I Am
By Ella Wheeler Wilcox

I know not whence I came,
I know not whither I go
But the fact stands clear that I am here
In this world of pleasure and woe.
And out of the mist and murk,
Another truth shines plain.
It is in my power each day and hour
To add to its joy or its pain.
I know that the earth exists;
It is none of my business why.
I cannot find out what it's all about,
I would but waste time to try.
My life is a brief, brief thing,
I am here for a little space.
And while I stay I would like, if I may,
To brighten and better the place.
The trouble, I think, with us all
Is the lack of a high conceit.
If each man thought he was sent to this spot
To make it a bit more sweet,
How soon we could gladden the world,
How easily right all wrong.
If nobody shirked, and each one worked
To help his fellows along.
Cease wondering why you came—
Stop looking for faults and flaws.
Rise up today in your pride and say,
"I am part of the First Great Cause!

119

> However full the world
> There is room for an earnest man.
> It had need of *me* or I would not be,
> I am here to strengthen the plan. "

I love her poetry very much and this seemed to sum up in a few words what I thought Tony felt.

Even as a medium Tony has never made contact with me. Maybe he's ashamed to talk but just as likely; he has found his Navy mates and is too busy talking over old times.

Prison humor was never far away. There's something about dire situations that brings out the funny side of life. I remember walking through the kitchen and seeing an inmate with a large green handled knife. The kitchen staff thought it odd that a man who stabbed his wife was given the job of cutting up the vegetables! This humor took a little getting used to.

Then there was a man who had held up a bank using a bottle of toilet duck (a brand that shapes its cleaner bottles to resemble a duck)! On his first morning in prison, as the inmates were being unlocked for breakfast, all I heard the sound of quacking coming from the landings. The other inmates only let him have boiled eggs as his first breakfast in a two-year sentence for armed robbery.

It was little things like this that cut through the boredom.

It was hard to keep anything secret; word soon spread that one of the officers worked as a medium. I didn't mind because if people were interested they could come and talk with me about their beliefs. I can't think of a place where you can meet so many different people from all sectors of the community in one place. It taught me not to judge a book by its cover, another lesson sent to me by spirit.

As I settled into prison routine I found I had time on my hands. I wasn't bothered about sitting in "The Box" (the control room on each landing). I would walk round and chat to the inmates. I got to know most of them and their stories of how they became caught up in the prison system. Some had never been out of prison since starting at a young age. They went from jail to jail. For them it was a way of life. It didn't matter which prison they ended up in; there was always someone they knew.

Then there were people like Colin, a middle-aged man who lived his life without doing anything wrong. He told me he had never even had a parking ticket before finding himself in court. Colin's story was very sad and brought home to me that prison wasn't always used to protect the public from dangerous criminals. Colin lived a normal life; he worked hard for many different employers. While working in a gentleman's club as a steward, he became addicted to the slot machine. He would stay late most evenings waiting for the members to go home while keeping a close eye on whether or not the £100 jackpot was won. This went on for months. The temptation grew and he would play the slot machine at any opportunity. This lead him to go more and more in debt. So he hatched a plan to play without losing. He obtained the two keys to unlock the back of the machine. This meant he could always get back what he spent by opening the back. As no records were kept of how much money went through the machine it was a failsafe idea. Colin failed to see the firm hold his gambling addiction had on his life. He lived to gamble. This went on for over four months.

He was finally caught, not taking money, but by chance. Another worker noticed the winnings were down and the finger pointed at Colin. Nothing could be proved but he, being of good character to that point in his life, owned up to everything. He caused his own downfall. He confessed by writing down everything he had done. Without his statement no one would have been the wiser. His bosses handed him over to the police, he was charged with theft and sent to prison for two months. He had only taken £800 but the judge made an example of him because of his breech of trust to his employer. (It had nothing to do with a lot of the judges drinking in this particular club.) So Colin found himself in prison without any support or help for his gambling problem.

The system let him down. I could tell he didn't fit into the normal prison population. When a man like Colin is sucked into the alien prison world, it sends a message to everyone. I liked him very much as he admitted he did wrong, never complained, looked after himself, stayed out of trouble and got through what must have been a life-changing experience.

People like Colin are not that rare in prison. I often thought that if the general public saw some of the reasons courts sent people to prison there would be an outcry. On the other end of the scale were hardened criminals; these men who had lived their lives in and out of prison. Once you've been in prison it's hard to start again. People often lose their house or accommodation, employment becomes a problem, ex-offenders find themselves caught between a rock and a hard place. If they apply for a job declaring their prison record many employers will pass over them. If they don't declare their prison record, they have to worry about being found out as it's a criminal offence not to declare. They could find themselves back in court and get sent back to prison.

Surely as a society we must help those who don't stand a chance. Do we really want to turn people into outsiders? I realize that some are hard-core people who could not care less. The prisons are full of bitter, hateful souls that our society doesn't know how to cope with. So we lock them up time and time again. Out of sight, out of mind.

I believe that our life is a learning process. We have to experience both sides to have a full understanding of the other person's viewpoint. That's how I met Andy.

Andy was a career criminal. He had been in trouble since he was eight. Now at the age of thirty he was starting to look back at the way his life had worked out. He would say to me "no way back for me gov" and he was right. Even if he had wanted to go straight he wouldn't have stood a chance in the world. The only world he knew how to survive in was prison. He had become instituted; his life set by the clock of prison routine, being told what to do and when to do it. He knew far more about prison than I would ever know. He knew every form, every job, how much he could earn in a certain time, even the grant he would receive on leaving prison. I found him an interesting person to sit and talk to. We both loved football; I often made a small bet with him on the outcome of a football match. It was only a Mars bar, not much for me, but for Andy it was a lot to lose. I went a whole season never losing. It became a standing joke each week as he handed over yet another chocolate bar. But give him his due, he always paid up. I still remember the joy on his face when he finally won. As I said before it's the little things that matter when you're locked up.

Andy was also very interested in the spiritual side of life. One thing you do have in prison is time. Time to think about everything. We would talk about life after death, past lives, heaven, and hell. Because he was so interested I decided to grant him a wish. Andy was after me for months for a personal sitting. I had refused because of the circumstances. My duty was to care for him. I had to consider how it might affect him; the smallest thing can send people over the edge. When you have no prospect of getting out, everything is magnified one hundred fold. In prison there are many rules, all for good reasons. But nowhere did the rules state that you couldn't sit with a prisoner in his cell and try to reach out for the other side of life.

The cells were tiny; just enough room for a metal-framed bed covered in brown sheets, a green bed cover, one chair, a table, wash basin, toilet with walls of light green and a small window three bars high opposite the large iron door. I turned my key and waited for the click. I disabled the door latch so I couldn't lock myself in. Other inmates would have found it very funny to lock me in; poetic justice in their minds!

I walked in. Andy smiled, pleased that I remembered my promise, "I didn't know whether you would turn up or not," he said.

"You know me, a promise is a promise."

I made sure he knew others were aware I was with him. They didn't know why but they knew were I was. My first rule

123

was never go off alone without telling someone where you were going and how long you would be. That held even with someone I trusted like Andy.

He sat on his bed. The harsh yellow light lit him up. I sat on the chair and looked directly at him. He was a small dark haired man with slits for eyes, his face pockmarked with old acne scares, dressed in a red and blue prison track suit. "Do you mind if I smoke gov?" he said taking out a small tin of rolling tobacco.

I nodded. I could see he was nervous and so was I. I normally shut down while working in the prison. Too many feelings rebounded and here I was open to them.

The connection was instant. I felt myself being taken to Liverpool, a place I'm very fond of and know well. But this wasn't anything nice. It was the scene of a murder. I watched as a young man fell to the ground. I could see the streetlights shine on wet greasy pavement. The man's name was Billy. It was Andy's brother who was killed ten years before in a street fight outside a club in Liverpool. I had no idea that was where Andy was from. Any accent was long gone.

Andy's face was white. The death of his brother affected his life in many ways. First, because it was his younger brother and Andy had looked after him from a young age. Andy was in prison the night Billy was killed. He felt guilty ever since. Billy was a real character. He showed me his blue Everton scarf, the knives he used to carry, one with an Eagle on the shaft, another with switchblade action. Andy confirmed that Billy always carried knives. They made him feel safe. He was involved in drug dealing; the streets of Liverpool weren't that safe.

Billy was able to make his peace with his brother that evening. The simple act of saying good-bye meant so much. Before moving on Billy had one final surprise for his brother. He told him about some money he had hidden in a safe deposit box two days before he was killed. He wanted Andy to have the combination so when he was released, the money would help him go straight. I gave him the five numbers and the location not believing what I was given. If the box was untouched and still there after Andy was released in two years maybe it was meant to be.

That reading went past the usual boundaries of trust between a prison officer and an inmate. Only three people knew of this; one was in spirit, Andy was inside for the next two years and I was free. Yet another test was sent from spirit. My thoughts were that I hoped that the money would give Andy a chance for a normal life. After all, his life wasn't going to start again until he was thirty-two. The cell came back into focus, the dull green walls, bright yellow light, Andy was stuck for words. I could see hope in his eyes for the first time. It would be a long journey over the next two years but I knew he would make it.

I can still see his face on the day he was released; he was scared and excited like a child waiting for Christmas day hoping for that one big present. The fear was it might not be there under the tree. I only heard from him once more. I got a simple note on the back of an envelope, sent to the prison, "Thanks Gov just like you said, Andy." I knew what it meant; I would never see Andy inside prison again.

Another prisoner I became close to was Bob. Bob had been in prison all his life. The courts often gave him custodial sentences because he was always breaking the law. He was a lovable rogue who could pick your pocket without you knowing it. He would tell me how he used to walk out of supermarkets with shopping carts full of drink unchallenged! He said if you had the nerve you could get anyway with anything!

I would just laugh at him and say, "If you were that clever, why did you end up in prison?"

He would smile and say he was in prison for something he didn't do--run fast enough! Bob didn't have any family apart from his friends inside so prison was home for him. One Christmas he had nowhere to stay so he got arrested for something petty, appeared in court the next day the judge freed him on bail much to his horror. So he jumped over the dock and punched the judge in the face. He was remanded for two weeks over Christmas in prison. He received a two-year stretch for assault shortly afterwards. He was proud of the fact the he was the only person in that court's history to give the judge a thump. The judge thought he was doing him a favor by letting him off.

Prison is full of people like Bob. You can't help but like him. I often wonder where you might meet someone like Bob other than in prison. The older officers remembered him as a younger man, always getting in fights. He once put two officers in hospital because they wouldn't let him make a phone call. But now, in his late forties, he was more manageable. Bob, more than anyone, opened my eyes to the real world. He's a person I'll never forget.

One of the more interesting things for me was working in an old building with so much history that included the stories of ghosts. Because I had a special interest, officers and inmates alike would tell me their experiences.

I heard there was a gray lady that floated legless above the floor in the corridor between the kitchen and the cook's changing rooms. There was an old condemned cell where the cooks changed into their kitchen whites. Now it was used as a storeroom, stacked high with tins and large sacks of flour and sugar. If you walked in there the feeling was very sad. It was a short walk to the hanging room which was closed down for good in 1956--only fifty years ago. I found it hard to believe that men spent their last moments on Earth walking down that passage way.

The story behind the gray lady was one of speculation and rumor. Prison officers working night shifts walked down the corridor patrolling between the main kitchen and the back of the prison. This duty was know as pegging because there was a clock every half-mile or so to make sure the officer did the duty. This recorded the time and date which created a record of the movements that night. If an officer missed a peg or was late it was taken seriously. So officers only missed a peg for important reasons. One night an officer come across the ghost of the gray lady. He forgot about his duty and ran back to the box, white as a sheet. Other officers went with him to investigate but nothing was seen and everything died down for a month. Then another member of the night shift staff saw exactly the same thing. A gray lady came floating down the corridor with no bottom half. So it was taken seriously.

I was asked if I could go with the patrol as I was the only officer who had training with spirits. I jumped at the chance. The other members of staff had mixed views. Remember these were hardened prisons officers who had seen many things, including strange goings on elsewhere in the main prison.

Before I go into a situation I like to know what I'm up against. So I did some research. I wanted to know if anyone else had reported seeing a gray lady in the back passage. I started with the duty log. I found logs that went back to the early part of the century; it took me weeks to go through them all. One 1906 report was of an incident that happened in the same corridor. A nurse working in the prison hospital was killed by scalding hot water. She was carrying a large urn that had fallen on her legs. She was alone at the time and her screams went unnoticed until a member of the night patrol found her close to death. She was taken to the hospital wing but died of terrible burns to her legs and shock. Was this the ghost of that nurse still haunting that area?

Having been on many visuals I knew that ghosts don't appear at will. I also knew that the area I was asked to investigate was very active. The men who were executed literally never left the prison. By law they were buried inside the walls of the prison. So much history in one place. So many had been through so much in this area alone.

Did the officers see the ghost of the nurse or gray lady?

I thought it was a replay ghost that was triggered by the conditions in the atmosphere and the officer walking past. As far as I know this ghost still appears from time to time.

During my time in prison I learned so more about people in six years than I would have in sixty years on the outside. All forms of life are found within the walls of a prison. It's the hardest job I've ever done, and when I left, I left a part of myself behind. I was one of the lucky ones who managed to escape; not many could or did. In my time working as a prison officer, I saw four inmates and two officers commit suicide, many others did harm to their own bodies that no person should ever do. I learned about drugs and the horrible toll drugs takes on lives. Over seventy five percent of the prison population was or had been on drugs. The pressure of working in this environment took its toll on the officers. Many turned to drink or had a nervous break down. Few prison officers lived a long life; the average officer retired at fifty-five and died at sixty-five. Ten short years.

I know spirit placed me in a position to learn what I needed. I wouldn't be the person I am today without having met people like Tony, Andy and Bob. When I walked through the gates for the last time I knew I would never go back, spirit willing.

I was moving to a new career as a counselor and a medium. I couldn't bear the thought of dying inside while going through the motions of a hollow existence and counting the days to retirement. Every time I stand on stage I think back to those days standing on the line trying to keep order and think to myself this is a piece of cake.

Chapter Nine

Leap in Faith

I feel privileged to be able to work the way I do. In fact I don't look at it as work. Work is stacking shelves, digging holes, or looking after people like the nurses and caregivers do. My work in the Prison Service taught me this. Being a medium is a full-time position. In my mind everything must be right for you to function properly. You must eat the right foods, exercise and not drink or smoke.

Not only do you have a duty to yourself, but a duty to spirit. Red Cloud told me early on, "You will tell many people many things most of which you will forget. No one will forget what you tell them."

I would pass that advice on to anyone who works as a link with spirit.

Over the years, I find that I am asked the same questions that I asked of my mentors, guides, and friends. I try to remember how I felt when I asked those questions. Red Cloud always answered a question with two more.

My very first question to Red Cloud when I first felt his presents was, "How can I help you?"

I knew it would be an exchange; his guidance for my earthly time. If I managed my time in working along side Red

Cloud I would find the answers for myself. The skill in being a guide is simple. Place the right thought in the right place. Red Cloud knew the questions I was going to ask because he placed the question to ask in my mind! This worked in many ways. Books stood out for me to read. I found myself talking to people for one purpose, only to discover months or years later the person was placed in my pathway for a totally different reason.

Red Cloud asked me, "How can you answer others questions if you haven't ask the same questions yourself?"

There is nothing that hasn't been asked before and won't be asked again. There is only one truth, yours. Find as many ways to your own beliefs as you can and stay flexible with an open mind and heart.

I now ask questions that are different than when I was in my twenties. I worried whether some one liked me. It bothered me if I heard bad things about anyone. If they can say that about them, they can also talk bad about me. Red Cloud showed me that people have free will to make their own judgments; nothing you can do about how others think. He taught me that how you form your thoughts is important. As I've gotten older I understand these words better. By thinking positive thoughts I attract positive thinking people towards me. These people ask positive questions that help me learn more about how I think. The spirit world is the essence of thought, so the nearer we get to perfection, the less we need the psychical body and the more thought plays a part in our existence? To understand spirit we have to think spiritually. How important are things like money, time, and opinion to us? If we can honestly answer that they are not important, then we have made our first step towards spirit. Again, to understand we must lose our human shackles.

When I answer questions for people I try to answer from a spiritual perspective, not a human one.

Here are some of the questions I have been asked during recent readings. Remember the truth I give is my truth, it might not be yours.

The first question that I found interesting was; "As a spirit returning for another life time, does that spirit fear they will have their soul and cell memory wiped clean? Is it starting all over again in a new life time?"

The first thing I acknowledge is that cell memory is always there, if we choose to access it. Soul memory is set much deeper, storing our understanding of life between lives. The idea of fear is a human emotion, not a spiritual sense. To place ourselves in spirit is to understand the need to learn about many human feelings such as, trust, and fear. So as a spirit we might choose to live a life that encompasses fear for many reasons but spirit wouldn't have a fear of learning those lessons. It's part of the process of the circle of life. We come from the light of love-energy and that's where we return once we grow enough to accept that we don't need a human body to exist; but we retain the memories of many life times in our spiritual consciousness. Each new incarnation is a new challenge, an adventure in time. As spirit we set our own path, we know what we need to do in any one lifetime to achieve the goals we set.

A spirit returning to Earth can choose the life they want to lead before hand. Whether it works out that way or not is up to the discussions that person makes while in human form.

I recently did a mediumship reading for a lady who watched her husband pass over from a crippling condition. She asked me an interesting question. "What would have happened if I had helped my husband commit suicide?"

I've often had people say to me that they weren't afraid of death, just the way they might encounter it. Taking your life is personal choice. It normally follows making many wrong decisions during that lifetime. In these circumstances the person is admitting to fail in that particular life. It may be pre-planned for that soul to experience the emotional pathways of a life like that. They have the choice to fight on or take a way out. By taking a way out they have an effect on the rest of their soul group. It is said that if a father takes his life the chances one of his children will follow that direction is much higher.

131

Add all the guilt, human pain, and anger that are left behind to that. Troubled human journeys take much understanding. In my personal view it makes it very likely that when the person passes back into spirit they will choose lifetimes with similar experiences again and again until they face up to finding a solution or make the choices that are different. That will lead to a different conclusion.

People who suffer towards the end of their life are no different. We choose to experience this emotional pathway whether it's a physical or mental illness. The spirit gives a chance to gather knowledge; for the person it's an impossible situation. It's even more so for the family who has to sit and watch helplessly. But when we do pass over we judge ourselves on lessons learned by placing our human form in this situation. The answer I gave the lady was simple, "It's choice. You have the choice to face or turn away, the chance to experience; learn or not. At some point these are lessons we all must go through.

Over my years as a medium, I've learned not to be judgmental in any circumstance; whether I'm talking to a person who just lost their lifetime partner of years or their pet budgie. While the example I give is extreme, the same rules apply. Treat every person with the utmost respect. When an old lady phoned me in the early hours the other day, her cat had just passed over to spirit. She was in a distressed state, reaching out for comfort from another human being. So I took time to explain that cats have a spiritual existence too. Many animals are here as life helpers and guides, true friends for humans during our dark moments. Animals give unconditionally and help many. That morning I was able to describe a large ginger tomcat in the arms of her late husband. The image I was given by spirit brought tears to my eyes and relief to a person who had lost a dear friend.

Spirit brings comfort to many through hundreds of mediums. You open a magazine and are hit by advertisements for a psychic or mystic or a medium. What is the difference between a psychic and a medium?

It's straightforward. A psychic claims to be able to work with a person on an individual basis. That person connects to your life, picks up on your personality, your past, and things you would or were thinking about doing and gives you direction into your future life. A rule of thumb that I use is: If the psychic can accurately show you where you have been and what's going on, they are likely to have a better chance of getting the future right. Remember that psychics are for guidance and not to make choices for you. Psychics work in a number of ways; by being with a person and linking in to their thoughts, divination cards, runes, sticks, tea-leafs, coins, and crystals. These objects help the psychic focus on you, seeing clearly (clairvoyance) your life path.

A medium is a mediator between the spirit and the human sides of existence, the bridge that makes communication possible. Mediums should be able to prove survival of the soul. To do this, credible evidence of the person who was and is now spirit again is most important. If you think as I do and believe in reincarnation, then your identity in one life is different to that in a previous lifetime.

Let me explain. If I went to a medium and my father came through the name he gave to the medium, it would only relate to the last life time we spent together. It would be far better if he came through with the personality he lived with during that period of his existence. Then I could relate to that information. In other words, the spirit that was my father is now only my father again in order to relate to the lifetime we shared. Mediumship can be very objective. It depends on the skill of the medium. Some things to watch out for when sitting with a medium are: Let them do the talking.

If the message is loud and clear a medium shouldn't have to ask, "Do you understand?" Or any other question for that matter. The best mediums trust spirit and pass on the messages they receive direct to you. After all, the message is for you and not them!

Out of the hundreds of calls for help I get, this one stands out; a person feels confused and doesn't know where to turn for help.

The lady's voice was loud and panic filled her emotions. "Can you tell me where I can find the psychic police?"

I had never heard of such an organization or if existed. "Why do you ask?" I asked back.

This lady believed someone had placed a curse or a hex on her. For her it was real. She saw her life as full of bad luck. She was desperate to change this and had looked up a psychic in her area. The psychic had told her that she needed to go to the psychic police without telling her where or how she would find them. She looked for their listing in the phone directory. When that didn't work she called her local police station, which seemed logical under the circumstances.

She was sure the police knew of the psychic police? The police gave her the telephone numbers of local psychics and mediums. They couldn't help her in any other way.

The first psychic didn't know how to talk to the lady about curses. It's not always easy to explain. However, as a medium I have a duty to help in the best way I can. I explained that spirit works through thought. If we believe in negative thoughts like curses, then the thought affects our beliefs. So we had to believe in the power of the negative first. This goes against universal law which is; love is the only real truth. The way forward is to send out loving thoughts to everyone starting with yourself. Affirmations work well. "I love and approve of myself," repeated morning and evening is a good start. If you don't like yourself, how can others love you? As for good and bad luck, I feel luck is an illusion that stops us from taking personal responsibility for wrong choices. It's easy to blame others for our short falls.

I met and talked with the lady for over four hours about the power of positive thought and choice. Although I was about to change her personal circumstances, I wanted to influence the way she thought. At first she was mistrusting, angry, very alone and isolated from the world by fear. By the time she left, she knew at least one other person in the world cared about her enough to make time for her. All it cost her was time.

One of my favorite sayings is "Little miracles happen everyday when you find spirit." That day was one of those miracle days.

Two weeks later I was going about my normal day-to-day routine when I heard a knock on the door. The lady was standing there with a big bunch of flowers. She looked at me, handed me the flowers and said, "Thank you so much," and shot off down the road. I knew then that she was going to be alright. She had turned her own life around. A personal miracle.

I believe what you receive is what you give out. That is why I never turn anyone away. In return many have helped me on my personal quest.

With this in mind, a close friend asked a question I think you might find it interesting: "Are there people on Earth who are programmed to help others?"

The short answer is, "Yes."

If you've come across such a person they know when to say or do the right thing at the right time. I believe that certain people can tune into your karmic record and guide you though some of life's minefields. So how do we recognize these helpers? There is no one way as we all have personal choice. If we choose to go it alone, we are not likely to listen or seek help. The first step is to open your heart and mind to others. The smallest kindness has the biggest impact on others and in return, on you. Be open to new ideas, ask questions.

I've found that people who are in tuned to others will find themselves in position to help others. A number of psychics and clairvoyants started their working life in service to others; nurses, chefs, hairdressers, and other helping professionals. The group is large and it is not just by chance. People with an ability to help others are normally placed in jobs that reach out to people. Nurses, the obvious profession, help others in time of need. People who handle food and practice healing are underestimated in our society. It makes sense that more evolved souls have had helping experience in many lifetimes.

I'm a great believer in positive thought. The more we think we can do, the more likely it will happen. The same applies to meeting people with the ability to influence our lives. The more we look, the more we find.

During my development as a medium I tended to stay away from development circles. While I feel it's a good idea to share, understand, and demonstrate on others, these circles were not a concept I felt comfortable with.

We all have different learning needs; we all work at a different pace. I've always been happy with my mentors and guides. Unlike most, they seem to swoop around and change as I learn new lessons every day. I can't remember standing still for one day.

You're only as good as your last reading. Improvement is always my goal. I've been fortunate with some of the situations that opened up in front of me. From an early age I met certain people at the right times. My early friendship with Katie, my grandfather George, then my own father, all had a huge influence on my own beliefs. Then John, who I met at the spiritualist church, my life in the Air Force and the prison service were all experiences that prepared me for the next step forward.

These were lessons I couldn't have learned anywhere else. I read many books written by worthy writers. I've been able to meet and exchange ideas with some of the best psychic minds and I have been challenged about my personal beliefs under intimidating circumstances. My belief structure is solid but not unmovable. We gather much knowledge from many sources. I like to stay open to these opportunities at all times. I find my own truth and don't repeat those of others. I'm never surprised to discover that much of what I still uncover was uncovered many times before by other generations.

Two of my closest friends were Victor and Hazel. Both were wonderful mediums with so much knowledge. Vic met Hazel before World War II. They fell in love just before Vic went off to war and spent nearly the whole five years apart. Vic was one of the last soldiers to be evacuated from the Dunkirk beaches; he told me what it was like watching German planes bomb the beaches and waiting for the next bomb to hit knowing it could be your last moment.

I used to think, "How soon we forget people like Vic and their sacrifice."

After coming back from Dunkirk, Vic went to fight across Europe facing life and death situations on a daily basis (and we talk about our lives being under pressure!). He ended up in Italy at the end of the war. He hadn't been home for over two years. While Vic was away in Europe Hazel had joined the land army; working twelve hours a day laboring on the farm to feed the country. Can you imagine people today doing what they did? Both were remarkable people in their own rights, but together made a very strong team.

After the war they married and ran their own company while exploring spiritualism. They set up their own spiritualist church to spread the word of spirit. I didn't meet them until they were both well into their late seventies. I have no doubt that I was placed with them to be taught the lessons they had both learned over their lifetimes. I owe them both so much.

Yes, developed into a stage medium, but without Vic's teachings it would have taken me a lot longer. He taught me everything from preparation before a sitting, how to address an audience, to knowing how to select the right person for the right message. We met by chance. Hazel had heard of my work through a mutual friend while recovering from an illness in a hospital. By pure chance, they were in the same place at the same time and talked about mediums. My name came up because a few weeks earlier I had done a photographic reading for my friend. (I can read people from a photograph. When I tune in it's like having the person in the room with me.)

Hazel wanted a reading but wasn't well enough to travel, so I was the solution. She phoned me and then sent me a photograph. I did the reading thinking nothing of it. Two days later the phone rang. It was Hazel; she was amazed at how accurate the photographic reading was and asked if I would do more readings for her family and friends. Over the next few weeks I did readings with the same results. We became firm friends up until her death in 2006.

She sent me up-to-date photographs of family and friends every year. I returned them with the taped reading. Hazel could never figure out how I knew so much about her life. I would smile at her and say she was an open book, which was far from the truth! I still miss her love and guidance. As a friend she was always waiting and wanting to help me move forward. When Vic died in 2005 after a short illness I knew Hazel wouldn't be far behind. They had been together for over sixty years; Hazel was in and out of the hospital for over five years before she passed on into spirit. The doctors said she was a walking miracle because she had escaped death on the operating table a number of times. When Vic died first it came as a shock to her. She thought she would be first to go. Her life was with Vic so without him she had little reason to fight on.

Hazel and Vic were the two most influential people in my learning and understanding of how spirit evolves. They taught me the purpose behind what I had always been, a natural medium. When I was with them I felt I belonged. They understood me because they went through everything I experienced. This was the first time in my life I felt I could talk openly about my feelings, beliefs and worries without being judged. This took some getting used to. From an early age I learned to hide my feelings from my parents, I was never shown any understanding.

Before Vic passed into spirit in 2005 he gave me a document. He said I would find it useful one day. This wasn't the normal writings of opinions and speculation. It was a full transcript of the messages he and Hazel received from spirit. It is an amazing read.

To give you a taste here is the first chapter; It's entitled *Life on Earth*.

Here follows several messages about *Life on Earth*, which is self-explanatory:

A child is conceived into your world on Earth in consequence of love, lust, adventure, or stupidity between two parties. A child of love has chosen its parents, mother, father, and the circumstances of life to come so that chosen path of spirit can be easily obtained. But results depend on the child when it reaches the age of free will. A child of lust chooses its mother with whom it can be born but it must remember that heredity is immaterial to spirit. The body is but the carrier of spirit. It is only the mind that is important; hence parents do not really matter. They affect date of birth and circumstances that enable the child to carry out its intended task on Earth in free will at a later age.

Therefore lust, adventure, and stupidity of the adults do not matter. What does matter are the circumstances that surround the child that is ultimately chosen. Of course, the mother bearing the child is slightly important in that she is able to introduce the child's spirit into the surroundings that were chosen. If the mother dies in childbirth or before the child's spirit grows sufficiently to fend for itself, then the child is protected by those around it or any other aura that is capable. If this is not so, then the child's aura is open to interference by lesser spirits. This may be the reason why so many of your young spirits find themselves in circumstances that are black or grey auras. They have unwittingly been overshadowed by those around them who are likewise. This is a severe test for the spirit involved, whether it remains as a grey or black aura or fights its way into the brighter colors of aura despite its surroundings.

A message received a few days before the one above also deals with the child.

And now my son, you have asked about when the spirit joins the newborn in your life on Earth. First, you know that the true body, the spirit body as you call it, is carried by the earthborn body while it is on Earth and leaves that Earthly magnetism when the Earth body ceases to function.

When the child is in the womb of its chosen mother, it is surrounded by the Earth body's aura-the mother. But as life progresses in the womb so it is building a magnetic aura around it, but as it has not met the Earth life, that aura is only of the physical.

When a child is born it holds a very fine (small) aura around it. Its physical magnetism is not very strong; this gradually extends to another aura-mental as the child progresses until it reaches about the age of seven Earth years by which time it is beginning to develop a spiritual aura of its own.

Up to this time the mother has encompassed the child with her spiritual aura.

But a child will often grow (if that is the correct term) a spiritual aura earlier than those seven years. As a baby with only the physical aura, it is open to be enveloped by spirit around it without the effort that we have to learn. That is reducing our vibrations magnetically to correspond with those on the Earth plane that we are use or communicate with.

For the child we reduce our vibrations as much as we can and so become visible to the children through their spirit eyes. You call it the third eye.

Nothing further has been received about the child entering the Earthly sphere. But there follows in as near sequence as possible to progression of life on Earth.

When we speak of "the spirit" we mean to refer to the spirit that has grown with the mortal during its time on Earth.

Let us explain:

When there is a choice to return to Earth, a minute part of the spirit soul is detached and joins the embryo of the unborn child. It has no other purpose than to grow into an outer body as the cells of the mortal grow. As the mortal grows cell by cell, each cell attracts an equivalent or matching cell plasma from the atmosphere of Earth.

Therefore it grows in rhythm to the growth of the mortal on Earth. In growing it reflects the experiences of that moral from inception to death on Earth.

When it leaves the Earthly body, because there is no longer an electro-magnetic attraction, it travels towards the original soul body from whence it came originally.

And so the soul body grows. And in growing accumulates the total experiences of all the spirits that have been on Earth.

Before leaving the thoughts and messages received from life on Earth, the three following messages have something to offer on the aspect of both life on Earth and spirit.

"There are many writings of those who will try to tell you how to live your lives when on the earth-plane. But are you aware that this group will not do so? In our opinion (yes we retain opinions on this side of the veil), living as an Earthly mortal is, to a large extent, individual.

The individual must choose how to conduct himself while on the Earth. He is given free will and has individual lessons to learn, experiences to overcome and a certain time on Earth to achieve it. So no other person can tell how another can live except in broad outline.

What we have set out to do, and are using you as our instrument on Earth to do it, is to describe as well as we are able, and so far as we are permitted, the transition from Earth back to the so called "spirit" world and the many intricacies that lie between being on Earth and returning."

One of the attributes of failure while on Earth is the almost unanimous failure of being impatient. Patience is an attribute which must be worked on while on Earth, for when the mortal returns to this world it must have infinite patience, both with itself and with others on both sides.

Let us explain:

When the chosen task is to communicate with mortals on Earth, we must have infinite patience in waiting until the mortal is ready to receive us in whatever form we wish to communicate. The delay may last many years while the mortal grows from birth, through the period of teaching and family. This before the mortal is in a position to be contacted.

It may happen sooner if we can find a way to 'open the door' with the mortal. Then, the choice to communicate with those on lesser echelons who have returned from Earth unprepared to accept this world may be on this side. It requires infinite patience to convince them.

These are few examples of patience required under certain circumstances. Once patience is learned and practiced, it follows that the satisfaction will develop into a fuller and happier life on Earth, and a greater purification of spirit here.

And Finally:

There comes a time in every mortal's life when they must look back on their lives on Earth and ask "What has been achieved while I have been here?"

There must be a purpose for having come to Earth and there must be satisfaction if that chosen task was achieved before returning to the true life on this side of the veil.

Ask yourself and others this question: "Do you think that your chosen task has been acted on and has it been fulfilled to the utmost of experience?"

It is not suggested that a return from Earth is contemplated for you or anyone around you. But the question must be put and the answer sought. We have to reflect on what we have set out to do and how far this task has been achieved before we can try to set out on further purification and achievement for that is the universal law of the universe."

I hope you found reading these extracts from Vic's writings as interesting as I have. The messages communicated from spirit have an insight that I believe to be greater than my own. And to tell the truth Vic and Hazel both sought for well over fifty years.

I miss them both terribly as in Vic's words 'as mortals'. But they both pop in from time to time for a chat and to catch up on the latest news. So Vic and Hazel, "Thank you so much for your love support and encouragement over the years. I will always value our time on this Earth plane together."

Chapter Ten

Inspiration

During the period of my life when I knew Victor and Hazel, we had some amazing discussions of a spiritual nature. Having listened to Vic talk about how the spirit body was infused with the mortal body, I was interested in the connotations of having two bodies; one on the Earth plane, the other in spirit. Was it possible to separate the astral body from the mortal one? I was soon to learn that you could do that in many different ways.

Our daily lives are normally far too busy for us to stop and look around. We carry on absorbing one experience after another. Our brains don't get a chance to process all the information gathered. So at night, when we slow down and sleep, it is an ideal time for the body to run all the information gathered in our subconscious back. Because this is a natural, everyday happening we take little notice of our dreams unless they stand out. Most of us forget what we were shown moments after waking.

I find that my personal dreams come in many forms. The most common is the mixed up dream that jumps around from place to place with no theme or reason behind why I'm placed into the situations. I have no control and when I wake have

143

little recall. These dreams are your brain trying to download all the information collected. I believe that everything we do or have done is recorded and stored in our cell memory. Dreaming is our natural way of storing this information. So when your dreams are non-scenic it's because they're not for you to make sense of. This is why we don't remember every detail.

The other form of dream that we lack control over is a nightmare. These dreams can be very real as they bring our fears to us. I remember having a nightmare after watching *The Wizard of Oz* as a child. The wicked witch of the north scared the living daylights out of me. I was only three or four at the time, but I still remember the fear I felt on waking up. I was right there with that witch and not a bucket of water anywhere to be seen!

Nightmares are brought on by a fearful or frightening experience. For me it was watching that film but for others it can be brought on by stress. Many soldiers have nightmares after being in battle. Posttraumatic stress triggers the mind into rerunning an experience time and time again. Fear is a powerful emotion. When we go through a fearful experience our mind is too busy trying to cope with the situation to be able store information. Survival is our number one instinct. Later, through dreaming, we can process what has happened. In life we have many lessons to learn. Overcoming fear is part of growing spiritually. Once you reach the understanding that death is not the end, fear is lessened. Nightmares are not very nice to experience but they help us face our fears. When we learn to trust fear we can reach our higher limits. Fear is a useful thing when we embrace what we fear. Our dreams help us recognize fears.

Reoccurring dreams are often triggered by our repeated behavior or by our thoughts and fears. To me it's because we hold onto the same concepts and do not move forward. As soon as we see that being stuck is based on our fear of making choices, doing nothing is better than making a wrong choice. We can make a decision, be it right or wrong, and the dream will cease. This is why we must look inside to find the answers to our uncontrolled dreams. We are often trying to avoid what we already know.

So far we have looked at dreams that can help us but we can't control. What if we could control our dreams? The possibilities are endless. We are only limited by our imagination. You can. It's called Lucid Dreaming. Frederik van Eeden was the first of many to do research into this form of controllable dreaming. Here is how to get involved:

The art of lucid dreaming is to be able to recognize that you're in a dream. Sounds easy doesn't it? Like anything else it takes practice and patience.

Lucidity typically begins in the midst of a dream when the dreamer realizes that the experience is not occurring in physical reality but is a dream. This realization is often triggered by the dreamer noticing an impossible or unlikely occurrence in the dream; such as flying or meeting the deceased. Sometimes people become lucid without noticing any particular clue in the dream; they just suddenly realize they are in a dream. A minority of lucid dreams are the result of returning to REM (dreaming) sleep directly from an awakening with unbroken reflective consciousness.

The basic definition of lucid dreaming requires nothing more than becoming aware that you are dreaming. However, the quality of lucidity varies greatly. When lucidity is at a high level, you are aware that everything experienced in the dream is occurring in your mind, that there is no real danger that you are asleep in bed and will awaken shortly. With low-level lucidity you may be aware that you are dreaming, perhaps enough to fly or alter what you are doing, but not enough to realize that the people are dream representations or that you can suffer no physical damage or that you are actually in bed.

Lucidity is not synonymous with dream control. It is possible to be lucid and have little control over dream content. Conversely, you may have a great deal of control without being explicitly aware that you are dreaming. Becoming lucid in a dream is likely to increase the extent to which you can deliberately influence the course of events. Once lucid, dreamers usually choose to do something permitted only by the extraordinary freedom of the dream state, such as flying.

You always have the choice of how much control you can exert. For example, you could continue with whatever you were doing when you became lucid with the added knowledge that you are dreaming. Or you could try to change everything-- the dream scene, yourself, other dream characters. It is not always possible to perform magic in dreams, like changing one object into another or transforming scenes. A dreamer's ability to succeed at this seems to depend a lot on the dreamer's confidence. As Henry Ford said, "If you believe you can or if you believe you can't, you're right." On the other hand, there appears to be some constraints on dream control that are independent of belief.

Lucid dreaming is a skill you can develop, like learning a new language. A few individuals may have an innate talent for achieving lucidity yet even they benefit from instruction and practice in making the most of their lucid dreams. More people experience lucidity as a rare spontaneous event but need training to enjoy lucid dreams at will. The best predictor of success with lucid dreaming is the ability to remember dreams. This, too, is a skill you can develop. With specific techniques, you can increase the quantity and quality of your dream recall. This in turn greatly increases your ability to have lucid dreams.

Lucid dreaming is a good way to start exploring the possibility of separation from the body, but it differs from 'Outer Body Experience' or OBE. Although we need to be relaxed and in a place were we won't be disturbed, we have total control of where we go during this time. This is how I practice this form of body separation.

First, I take the phone off the hook and place a Do Not Disturb sign on my door. Make sure you have at least an hour. Then either sit in an upright position in a chair or lay on a bed.

Now close your eyes, count to one hundred nice and slow, then breathe in on the count of five hold the breath for a count of five then breathe out again on the count of five. This should relax your mind and calm your body into a relaxed state. Repeat this process five times.

Now with your eyes closed, picture the room you're in. Note object colors, where items are placed and only in your mind, get out of the chair or off the bed and see yourself walking towards the door. Open the door, look around, notice everything, note whether you feel hot or cold, feel door handle as you touch it and ask how it feels?

Now walk around your house but only in your mind. Notice the smells in the different rooms as you pass through. Now get your shoes and a coat if you need one, open your front door and remember to lock it. Now you're outside your house. Look around, feel if it's sunny or rainy, notice the sky, the people you might meet on your walk and make a mental note of who you meet. Still walking, go to a place you might find yourself going to in your daily life. It can be a shop, the park or your child's school but it has to be an easy walk from your home. (Your mind should be focused so you feel you are really there.) Find a park bench or a place to sit where you can rest and look around. If you want, pick up a stone and write your name on the pavement. Or pick daisies in the park. Again take in everything from the colors to the feel of the wind in your hair, your legs might even ache, your throat may be dry or the walk may have made you feel tried. Take in everything you see, feel, hear, taste, and sense. It's time to return home. Repeat the journey in reverse. Open your front door with your key, walk through the house to the room where you are, open the door and sit back in your chair or lay down on the bed and open your eyes. You might need to give yourself enough time to find your bearings. Now for the interesting part. You are now fully aware and wide awake; I want you to repeat your journey step for step but this time for real. Notice everything that you saw in your mind. Compare it. Is your real journey the same or different in any way? Walk to the place where you picked your flower or wrote your name. Is it as you remembered in your mind? Is your name written on the pavement? Are there flowers missing? Do your legs ache? Is your throat dry? This takes practice, but if you stick to it you will find that you can travel further and further until you have no limits.

I know people who used this technique to visit family friends and destinations all over the world. The only limits are you and your imagination.

Astral travel is also much spoken of. This occurs when, during sleep or meditation, the 'astral body' leaves the 'mortal body' and travels to the astral plane to meet spirit guides, family members even review their life plan.

I have done a lot of research in this subject. It is fascinating and has had many positive results.

I first got into astral travel years ago when I felt I had the experience of leaving my body and floating off. It was an odd state to be in because I knew I was not in my body and was floating. Yet, at the same time, until I consciously gave it thought, my state of mind held out. It's a bit like when you know you are daydreaming but if you think about it the daydream ends.

Years after my first experience I decided to use meditation to go into a state of astral travel. This seemed to work. Then I decided to experiment with the possibility of making myself visible in another location. While going into the state one day, my mind wandered off on its own. I found myself in the room of a friend who was aware that I was there. He called to find out what I was doing. I found this interesting because not only did I feel like it had happened, but someone phoned me and confirmed what went on. I found it difficult to get myself back into that state of mind, as my conscious mind would interfere. Over the next few years I did similar tests where I went to my friend's workplace, reported what I saw and compared notes.

After a number of years doing this myself, I decided to try guiding a friend into the state of mind required. This created interesting results. I noticed movement around my friend at the time he left his body and re-entered his body. He reported where he went, what he saw and when we checked this it was accurate.

The most effective way to achieve astral travel is to learn to relax totally and free your mind of all thought. Then sense leaving your body and instinctively know where to go. Just go with the experience. If you begin to consciously interfere it will be difficult. If you know how to drive a car then try to pay full attention to what you are doing as you drive. You will find it is harder than driving instinctively.

Remote viewing is another from of OBE.

In the late seventies the American government used psychics to spy on other countries using remote viewing. A psychic was given a map reference and asked to describe the area and what they saw at that location. A man named Adrian Morehouse was chosen to lead a team of American psychics for the CIA.

The results were astonishing considering that the American government denies using remote viewing experiments. Morehouse openly came to the public and described the results as outstanding. It was amazing that an American government official admitted to remote viewing. He said it was true and was used successfully for espionage.

One story told by Morehouse was of a group of three remote viewers that were given map grid references of an underground complex. The American government knew it existed but did not know or could not prove what it was used for. They felt it too dangerous to send Special Forces to investigate. So Morehouse and his team were given the task of determining what was there. All three psychics came back with the same information; the complex was an underground prison. This is one example of the military value of remote viewing.

I learned to use remote viewing techniques to look for lost objects. Not long ago I found a missing dog by tuning into the map of the area. Here's how it works for me: I put a photographic picture of the place in the center of my mind. It's like having a camera strapped to your head with the image being beamed back to your thoughts. I was able to describe the area and direct the owners to the location of their dog. I have found all sorts of things using this method. All I need is a photograph of the missing object (or a detailed description so I can build a picture in my thoughts) and a grid reference that can be obtained from a local map. The Internet is a big help in providing quick, easy access to photos and maps.

With all the pieces in place I start my search. I have found many things over the years including a diamond ear ring worth over seven thousands pounds, countless passports, coins, lost wills, birds, cats, dogs, missing people and one time I found a missing child. That amazed the police. Remote viewing is linked into psychometry. This is the skill of being able to hold an object and sensing an imprint of the history of the object. I was lucky enough to hold a medieval window frame recently in my home City of Norwich, It was unearthed in my local hairdressers. Here's the story:

Norwich has a rich city history. Some of the oldest parts reach way back in time. This leaves an imprint in the shops and homes that look so familiar to us that we hardly notice what lies below the surface.

One such area is St Augustine's. It's just north of the city center. The street dates back over six hundred years to the fifteenth century. Stroll down the street with the smell of traffic fumes in your nostrils and large advertising signs catch your eyes. They may distract you from some of the smaller shops set back from the busy main road.

One such property is a hairdressing salon called Trends. Walk into this modern shop and you hardly realize the history in the building: You encounter the smell of hairspray, high backed red leather chairs, sinks and the staff busy cutting hair; the chatter of conversation, friendly atmosphere, a welcoming place where I had been many times in the past. I never really gave what was above my head a second thought or wondered of the history that was there.

The building has stood for over six hundred years. That is quite remarkable when you think of all the changes the property has seen. Imagine the tales we would hear if it could talk. The current owners recently decided to restore and expand upstairs. The builders got permission from listed buildings trust to reconstruct the floors, walls, and ceilings. While carrying out this work, they unearthed a medieval window frame hidden behind a wall for hundreds of years. This was our key to the past. Using psychometry, these large black dirty pieces of timber could share secrets of the past six hundred years.

But first, we were in for some surprises in the room below.

When you walk towards the end of the shop floor, open a concealed door, climb old narrow wood stairs, peer around a corner and you see a partition wall made from fruit boxes. This gives you a clue to the history back to pre war times. The shop then was a greengrocer. The smell of wooden oranges still strangely hung in the damp air.

This room had the feel of women working weaving baskets. Looking up at the uncovered ceiling you saw orbs jumping around the roof space leaving a light trails behind them with blues, greens and yellows mixed up together. The energy was very powerful. You could sense the movement of past occupants almost willing us to make contact. I would have loved to stay longer but this wasn't the time. Another day I thought.

Moving reluctantly, I opened another narrow door revealing a similar staircase. I thought of the different people who have climbed these stairs. I wondered what I would find. To my amazement I was hit by a very bright calm room; no feeling of sadness or repression, just peace. Looking around I saw newly laid plaster on the walls, the ceiling not yet in place, the old walls still had reeds sticking out with a sense of history all around. My attention was drawn to a pale blue plastic bag; out of place in its surroundings. Inside laid the four large pieces of black crumbling timber that once made up the frame of a very heavy window. This is what I had come for; a chance to be able to hold and feel the history of this unique time capsule psychometry would unlock.

I grasped a large piece of the old oak window frame and the wood crumbled between my fingers. I closed my eves and started to concentrate.

My head filled with noise; people shouting at the top of their voices. I heard water rushing past, and then felt the presence of a tall, slim dark haired man with jet-black hair, a dark beard, and sunken eyes. He was dressed in dark clothing. He was the property owner when it was built. It was like being drawn back into history; a world a million miles away from the one we inhabit.

Then the smell of fire and the sound of loud explosions filled the air. It drew me into a state of fear, people running, crying, shouting; then nothing but calm. Opening my eyes I saw Andre and Cherry, the current owners, looking at me. I was only away for a few minutes. It felt like centuries. I placed the old oak timber back into the pale blue plastic bags and thought I must do this again soon.

The experience knocked me back a little; I hadn't expected that much from a shop I had visited many times in the past. The upstairs floors were very active, the spirits of the past were part of the building; trapped in time waiting to be discovered. We were given a tiny glimpse of the past, a privileged look back.

I will never sit in those high backed red leather chairs again not knowing that just above my head is so much history waiting to be explored.

Psychometry can unlock so much. I believe the imprint that history makes is at our fingertips. Why not try for yourself? Old coins are a good start. Think of the different hands they have been through! You will need a pen and paper to record your findings.

Relax your mind just as you would before meditation. Breathe in on a count of five, hold for three, then breathe out on a count of five. Repeat this five times. This allows you to clear your thoughts and concentrate on the object. Hold the object in your weak hand, e.g., if you're right handed place it in your left. Use your strong hand to write your thoughts down. Listen to the first things that come to your mind. You may have to be quick as the images can jump around. Write as much as you can. With practice this can be fun at parties; especially if the object you hold has a history known to its owner. The more you get right the easier it becomes to trust what you feel.

Like much in life, we have to learn to trust our instincts first, then that of others. Should we trust our dreams? Are they mixed up emotions that we haven't worked through? Or are they hidden meanings?

Last night I dreamt about robbing a bank! I couldn't believe I had done something so stupid. I knew I would be caught and sent to prison for many years. I spent the rest of the dream running from the police and woke up feeling exhausted. Does this mean I will rob a bank in the next few weeks? No way. But perhaps the dream goes deeper into my sub conscious. I fear returning to prison where I worked for many years, only this time as an inmate.

This means my dreams are very personal to me and my situation. I don't believe that my guides are sending me a message. But what if some dreams predict the future? How would we recognize the difference between subconscious fear and future predictions? The simple truth is that we can learn to listen. In our everyday life we are bombarded by a lot of different information. We hold onto what we want to acknowledge and let go of what we want to dismiss. Why should dreaming be any different?

Prophetic dreams, also referred to as precognitive dreams, are dreams that seem to foretell the future. One theory to explain these phenomena is that our dreaming mind pieces together bits of information and observations that we normally overlook or that we fail to consider. In other words, our unconscious mind knows what is coming before we consciously piece together the information. Remember there is no time in spirit. If spirit wants to make contact with us through dreaming, it's likely to be in the form of a precognitive dream.

I have found these dreams to be far clearer than our normal dream state. Another thing that stands out is that we are far more likely to remember the dream when we awaken. If you experience a prophetic dream, write it down and post it to yourself. This confirms at a later date, that you received that information on the day the letter was postmarked. There is no point in being wise after an event if you knew what was going to happen.

I did this after I received a dream telling me an asteroid was going to hit the mainland in South America. The dream came true a few days later. I believe that these types of dreams are very common and are connected to claircognizance (universal knowledge). Everything that ever was is available for us to receive if we open our minds. Dreaming is one of the ways we receive this knowledge. Think of the implications for the human race if we all took notice of precognitive dreams. Many inventors, musicians, and writers have had ideas placed in their dreams. This brings the links between this plane and the spirit plane closer.

Doctors have tried to explain Near Death Experience or NDE for many years. People have found themselves floating above their bodies before being drawn back down. If we take the scientific approach, it should not happen. But so many have experienced this that something must happen. I spoke with a down-to-earth man the other day. He had no particular belief in God or religion but nearly died on the operating table. He felt his consciousness being lifted out of his body. He was fully aware of the chaos below as nurses and doctors fought for his life. They succeeded and he survived. But it made him look at life a lot differently; it was just hard to come to terms with. I have spoken with medical staff that place objects or words high above operating tables just in case. To my knowledge no one has returned after a NDE with answers. But I have no doubt something real happens. It is not that different from astral travel or remote viewing. Humans have the abilities to not only leave the mortal body but also to control how we use this knowledge. It depends on whether or not we have the patience to learn the techniques required. If we endeavor to open our minds to all the possibilities, we can enhance our lives in ways we could only dream of.

Throughout this chapter I have talked about many forms of disconnecting the spirit body from the mortal body. When we pass into spirit this is the alternate journey. We leave our mortal body behind as a shell. It's just the vessel that holds our soul. As Vic described in the last chapter, the magnetic field breaks and releases the soul. The body can be old, worn out or damaged so why would we want to keep that body for future use?

This raises the question of cryogenics. This is the science of freezing the body after death in the hope that one day medical science will be able to bring these bodies back to life and full fitness.

A long-standing urban legend maintains that Walt Disney was cryogenically frozen and his frozen body is stored underneath the Pirates of the Caribbean ride at Disneyland. However, Disney was cremated and the first known instance of cryogenically freezing a body occurred a month later in January 1967.

Why would we want our mortal body retained for future use? Ever since the beginning of time man has reached for immortality. Cryogenics is another way of trying to reach that goal.

If you have a spiritual belief in the soul leaving the body at the point of death, there is no need to hang onto an old body because we will be given a brand new one when we reincarnate into our next life time.

Chapter Eleven

Heavenly Beings

Throughout my life there were many times when I have felt very alone, even with my guides and mentors close at hand. They seem to disappear when the big decisions needed to be made. I'm sure this is true for most mediums. I remember talking to a well-known medium who felt exactly the same way. It's because we all make mistakes by ourselves. Every time I have a problem I need to call on my guides, mentors or even Katie to help me find the answers. What would I learn if others took the responsibility for making my choices? I understand guides taking a back seat even if it's hard to cope with being left in silence. My guides taught me this lesson at the age of five.

I'm still learning that lesson four decades later. I still think we all need support from time to time and angels are easy to call on. But what are angels? I think of them as heavenly beings or energy that we can summon for help and guidance. As I explained in chapter 3, when I work as a medium and especially on stage, I feel them swirling in all around me. They connect the souls from spirit to the mortal souls on this plane. I wouldn't be without my angels. But how can angels help us in our everyday life? Sometimes we need help for the little things.

I have a friend who asks his 'parking angel' to find him parking space whenever he goes into London. It nearly always works! I do a similar thing when driving on busy motorways. I ask my angels to make sure the slippery roads are clear. Try it for yourself. In your life, the little things make the difference.

What are Earth angels?

Earth angels are people who chose to live their life in service to others. They seem to have the happy knack of being in the right place at the right time. During World War II many stories were told of soldiers surviving by being pushed out of the way of mines and shells by someone they never saw or met before, but who was with them at the right moment. One story that sticks in my mind was of a young private fighting in the trenches in World War I. He was sitting at the bottom of the trench on a wooden box having a smoke and a drink. A lady dressed in a nurses uniform came around the corner and asked him if he would help carry some medical supplies. He gladly agreed. He got a hundred yards down the trench when a shell exploded in the trench he had come from. He would have been killed. Counting his blessings he turned round to find no sign of the nurse. He looked everywhere, asking anyone he found if they had seen the lady in the gray uniform. Not only had she vanished, but no one had seen her. Was this an Earth angel?

Another story I heard was of a young girl who didn't know whether or not her boyfriend was going to stay with her. Driving to work on a busy motorway she asked her angels for guidance. She asked them to send her a sign. Would they would stay together and get married? She had just finished asking when a large truck with her boyfriend's name written all over it drove in front of her. Needless to say they stayed together and got married a year later. Was this her angels showing her what was going to happen or was it pure coincidence? I think if you ask your angels they will guide you.

Here are some stories given to me from people all over the world. The first is from Vera who lives in Perth Western Australia.

This happened several years ago. I was working as an early morning cleaner. I woke at 4:00 a.m. and got ready to leave by 4:30 a.m. My husband is a shift worker and was on the afternoon shift so he was sound asleep, or so I thought, as I ventured out to my job.

When I left each day I locked the front door, lifted the garage door, started the car up, reversed, got out of the car, pulled the garage door down and drove away.

This particular morning, I locked the front door, lifted the garage door, started the car up, reversed, and for some unknown reason, I decided not to get out of the car to pull the garage door down. I drove to work without problem. But, when I got home I saw my garage door smashed to the ground!

My husband's account is this: He heard me start the car; reverse down the drive, then he heard a huge bang! He ran to the front of the house thinking I had hit something. He found the garage door on the ground.

I believe that when I got to the bottom of the drive the garage door caved in. Why didn't I get out of the car that morning as usual? You decide.

I wish to add this: The guy who replaced the garage door told me, "I've been in this business for over twenty years. Of all the garage doors I've replaced, they've collapsed from one side of the wall. Yours collapsed from both sides of the wall. So if you had pulled the door down, you would be dead."

This is a true account of what happened to me.

These words of Vera's made me think how precious life is.

This next account comes from America:

A few years back, my family and I went to see a movie. To leave the movie, you go down about ten to fifteen stairs. I fell on the first one and out of nowhere an older woman helped my spouse helped me up.

When we turned to thank her she had disappeared into thin air. She was nowhere to be found. I don't know about you, but I say she was my guardian angel, lending a helping hand. Not much to tell, but my family and I were shocked that she disappeared so quickly.

Janice M. - Alabama, USA:

This story reminded me of the solider in the trench. I began to wonder just how common these experiences are. I'm sure we are guided to the right place at the right time; this story confirms my belief:

This was sent by The Reverend Tom Birch from Norwich England. The words are his own. After fifteen years, this story can harm no one. In fact it may inspire all who read it:

It was early on February 1, 1992. I was staying with my wife and saw what I can only describe as three angels. They were with me in the bedroom. They said nothing but I got the distinct impression that they needed my help. Taking care not to make a noise and wake the cat, I got out of bed. I dressed without knowing where I was supposed to go, tiptoed out the front door and found myself heading home over two miles away. As I came to the foot of the hill just short of my house, I looked at my watch. It was 3:00 a.m. All I needed to do was cross the road opposite a pub. As I crossed I heard angry shouting. I turned to see a young man running down the hill. As he reached me, he backed himself against the wall of the pub to face his enemies. A gang of five came in hot, threatening pursuit.

I heard the angels in my head say 'go'. I had help this young man. That is why I was brought to this location in the dead of night. I didn't think of the danger; I just ran over to the young man and embraced him just as the gang leader arrived and smashed a fist into the man's face. Blood splattered all over my face and shirt; but the mob didn't know what to do with this old man in the way. Instead of continuing the beating they drifted off. I took the young man the few yards to my house and phoned his family. They were surprised to hear from me but relieved that their son was okay apart from a bloody nose. It would have been worse if the angels hadn't pointed me in the right direction or if I had not listened.

Tom adds this as a footnote;

A poem by D. H. Lawrence

What is the knocking?

What is the knocking at the door in the night?
It is somebody wants to do us harm!
No, no. It is the three strange angels.
Admit them. Admit them'.

That night Tom was open to listening. He was glad he was but would we all hear when called upon?

These next angel experiences were told to me by Lizney Goodchild who lives in Essex England.

As a child Lizney would see the devil. This started when she was only four years old. Her bed would shake and she would curl up in a ball too frightened to call out. This happened most nights. In her mind she asked for help never thinking it might come in the form of four angels. One night she went to bed expecting the bed to shake but it didn't. She was surprised to see her room lit by a bright but gentle light. Getting the courage to look over the sheets she was amazed to see four angels, each holding a corner of her bed. For the first time in months she felt safe.

Describing the angels as slim, in light pale robes, illuminated in a soft golden light, with fair hair, they positioned themselves with their backs towards the bed. They held the corner with arms and hands pulled behind their backs. She only saw one a female who would turn and smile at her. This made her feel calm. Lizney still remembers the white light that enveloped her during these visits. What's more remarkable is this wasn't a one off experience. It went on for five years until she was nine. The bed stopped shaking and her night angels faded away. But this wasn't the last angelic contact for Lizney. She would pick up telepathic messages often having thoughts placed in her mind. She always knew she would work along side spirit; this was her angel's way of protecting her.

When Lizney was around nineteen she had another experience with a different type of angel.

This angel was male, eight feet tall, dressed in Egyptian clothing with a long gold chain round his neck and a medallion hung just above his belly button. Dark olive skin, large brown eyes, which shone brightly, the whites around the eyes were extra bright, they almost glowed with short cut dark black hair. Most noticeable were his wings, made from light energy. They shimmered transparently with electricity, glowing all the colors of the spectrum. He communicated telepathically giving off a sense of well-being.

Lizney now in her early fifties had followed her dream of working with spirit. With her angels by her side she always felt safe.

People often experience angels when a member of the family comes close to passing over. This next story comes from Linda Peters from Belfast, Northern Ireland.

Linda's mother was ill. No one knew quite how ill but the family was worried. Linda, who was especially close to her mother, had a sinking feeling in her chest. You know the feeling you feel when you 'know' that something difficult is about to happen. On the morning when her mother went to see a consultant, Linda experienced what she described as a 'giant angel' that manifested in front of her. He was around eight feet tall and took up most of the space in her living room. It was surreal, like a waking dream, but she felt calm and peaceful for the first time in months. She wasn't worried about her mother even though the thought of being without her scared the life out of her.

When she returned, the news wasn't good. Her mother had cancer. The doctors were kind but that didn't alter the fact that her life was coming to an end. Sixteen weeks later, the angel appeared to Linda, this time in her bedroom. Linda knew that her mother didn't have much longer but again, she felt calm. Peace filled her head. There was no panic only knowledge that her mother was safe with the angels.

When I talked with Linda, I had no doubt that without the help she received from her heavenly being she would never have coped with the passing of her mother. The vision of the angel standing in front of her, not once but twice, was a moment that changed her life.

I'm very grateful to John from Derby England for this next tale of extreme strength. Was this an angel that helped him in his hour of need?

John was disabled. Most of his adult life he was confined to a wheel chair but despite his disability John lived a near-normal life. One cold icy morning he left his home with his wife for a short journey to the shops. It was just another day. She often pushed him along the narrow path that runs alongside the steep riverbank. This morning they were laughing and joking about brass monkeys when John's wife slipped on black ice and lost control of John's chair. It started to slide down the riverbank. It went fast at first, then slowed up in the reeds just before the riverbank. John could feel his chair sinking in the soft ground and knew if something didn't happen and happen fast, he was going for a swim. The a young man appeared from nowhere, waded down the bank, picked up John and his chair and carried them back up the bank to safety. John was no small man; in fact he weighed over twenty stone. So lifting him and carrying him and his chair up a steep slope was a feat of extreme strength. The fair-haired man placed him back on the footpath without saying a word and walked off in the direction he had come from.

John and his wife were amazed at what had happened. His wife stood rooted to the spot staring as John sat in his chair. They never made it to the shops that day.

Was this man an angel? Or was he just a very strong young man who happened to be in the right place at the right time? We might never know but what we do know is that without his help John have lost his life that morning.

My last story comes from a lady who I'll call Mary.

Mary lived in a house on the edge of Dartmoor, a remote area in the southwest of England. She got used to people knocking at her front door asking for help in one way or another as they walked across the moor.

One Sunday morning Mary cooked her Sunday roast and was about to sit down with her husband to eat. She heard a loud knock at her front door. When she opened the door, she saw a man in a brown jacket, blue jeans with a light colored scarf wrapped round his neck. He looked tried so Mary invited him into her home and offered the grateful stranger a meal. The man accepted with a smile. Mary couldn't help noticing the man's prefect white teeth and deep blue eyes. Over lunch he told them about his journey. He was an odd-job man looking for work. He traveled the length and breadth of the country looking for work. Although the man seemed genuine, his story didn't fit. His hands were soft and white, fingernails nicely trimmed, his complexion was light and not at all weather beaten from working outside. But he was polite and very knowledgeable. Mary didn't mind who or what he was, she had plenty of food.

The man finished his meal, helped Mary and her husband wash up, then with a hug, he put on his coat and scarf began to leave. By now Mary was wondering just who her unexpected guest was.

She wondered because as he left he said, "By helping many you could just have helped an angel."

His words bounded around the hallway as the man walked out of the garden and disappeared into the late afternoon.

Was this man an angel looking to test Mary? All we can do is look at the facts. Some years later Mary is convinced she shared her dinner table with a heavenly being. Who am I to say she didn't?

I believe that angels touch many lives. People from all over the world have experienced truly life-changing moments. As I always say, "Little miracles happen every day."

Are angels the only heavenly beings that we come across during our mortal life on this planet? Somehow I doubt it. The next two stories come from a different prospective. Make up your mind whether or not you feel these encounters were with angels or not.

This first story happened when I was in my twenties. This is the first time I have gone public with this experience.

It was a normal day. I got up early to travel to London. I had arranged to meet an old friend to discuss a work project.

We agreed to meet in a hotel in the center of the city, then go for dinner in the evening.

I always arrive an hour before my scheduled meeting time as I hate being late. I picked up a copy of the morning newspaper to pass time. As I read, I became aware of a man sitting across the hotel lobby from me. He was slim, tanned, had no hair or eyebrows, a small narrow mouth and deep blue eyes. I sensed him watching me, so in my head I said if you can hear me scratch your nose with your left hand. With his left hand he slowly scratched his nose. I was shocked. Was he reading my thoughts? If he was he could now feel my fear. I would accept any response. I decided it may be a coincidence. So, instead of asking him to do something simple I asked him to walk over to the reception desk, wait for the count of ten then go back and sit in his seat crossing both legs, right over left, then left over right. He followed my instructions to the letter. I knew that we had telepathic contact. Now my fear was gone and I was excited. What did he want from me? Why had he sought me out in a busy hotel lobby in the center of London? I had so many questions. But the first one that came into my head was "Who are you?"

"Michael," came the instant reply.

"Are you an angel?" I asked.

The thought came back, "You could say that I'm from a different realm."

I was sitting over ten meters away and too scared to think. Michael picked up my thoughts.

I should have gone across the room and embraced this stranger. But fear took over. I looked away, looked back and he was gone. It only took a tenth of a second.

I often think back to that time. What I would do if given that opportunity again? I get no second chances.

I'm sure Michael was not human. I'm also sure he sensed my fear and that's why he didn't stop.

The experience of being in the presence of Michael changed the way I think about the universe. I always knew that many life forms populate the cosmos. I now had my proof and I keep this years later.

Heavenly beings come in many different forms. I remember sitting down to meditate one morning. It was my normal routine before work. I clear out any personal thoughts and tidy my mind, ready to receive messages from spirit.

This morning I went though my normal routine of climbing high up inside my hollow oak tree. On reaching the top I walked out in my meadow and sat down beneath the young apple tree that I planted the first time I ever meditated. It had grown into a mature tree with large red apples. I looked in wonderment. It brought joy to my heart. I loved going to my secret place. It was mine. Nobody in the world would disturb me. I would guard it with my very existence.

So you can imagine my surprise at sitting quietly when a voice popped into my head. This wasn't my guides or mentors. The voice and presence was different; a smooth north east English accent, our conversation went like this,

"Please tell me your name"

"JOHN."

"Thank you John do I know you?"

"MAYBE YOU HAVE HEARD OF ME."

"Are you family?"

"NO."

"What would you like to talk about?"

"LIFE FAMILY FRIENDS WOULD LOVE TO TALK TO MY PEOPLE."

"Who are your people?"

"YOKO SEAN JULIAN MY FAMILY SO MUCH TO SAY."

"John when you said I might know you I think I do. Are you John Lennon?"

"WELL DONE."

"John why now?"

"JUST TAKEN THE OPPORTUNITY TO MAKE GOOD MY PROMISE."

"What promise was that?"

"TO SHOW THAT NOTHING COULD F--KING STOP ME."

"What would you like to say?"

"TWO FLYING TWO NOT,"

"Two flying two not what does that mean?"

"PEOPLE WILL KNOW,"

"What people?"

"THE OTHERS,"

"JULIA, FRED STILL AT SEA NEVER EVEN SEEN HIM COME BACK."

"Who are Julia and Fred?"

"MUM AND DAD, MEN LOVE STREET, JULIA WALKS NOW."

"John, that doesn't mean much. What would you like me to do?"

"PASS IT ON."

"Okay I will try but I can't promise,"

"AUNT M, SHE IS HERE."

"Who is she?"

"A VERY STRICT WOMAN WHO MADE MY LIFE HELL WHO I RESPECT, HELPED ME GROW UP."

"So a very important lady will let the others know who that lady is."

"OH YEA."

This was my first contact with John Lennon, a few days later John was already waiting for me,

"John, please tell me when you were born?"

"FORTY."

"Is that it?"

"YES."

"Please Tell Me Where."

"NORTH OF ENGLAND."

"John what would you like to talk about?"

"YOKO STARS ARE AROUND JUST LOOK YOU MUST LOOK DON'T LOOK DOWN CATH JULIAN NO BACKING UP GO FORWARD, SEAN YOU REALLY ARE

A STAR ALL BY YOURSELF. TWINKLE TWINKLE LITTLE STAR HOW I WONDER WHERE YOU ARE."

"What do you mean?"

"SEAN WILL UNDERSTAND."

"Hope So."

"GEORGE SLEEP WELL WE WILL MEET AGAIN."

"Do you want to add?"

"Do you have? Something else?"

"YES FOR YOUR THOUGHTS OF HOPE, THOUGHTS OF LIFE,

WHATS HAPPENS HAPPENED NO TURNING BACK,

STEP BY STEP, SLIDING BY NEVER STOP LISTENING,

WHY;WATCHING OUT FOR EACH OTHER,

NOT RUNNING FOR COVER,

STAND UP AND BELIEVE NOT TO CRY,

JUST KEEP ASKING WHY,

WHAT HAPPENS HAPPENED NO TURNING BACK,

TIME SLIDING BY."

"OK Would you like me to pass that on?"

"YES PLEASE PASS THIS ON

PLEASE LISTEN THIS IS CALLED BROKEN SKY,

IN A MISTY MORNING AFTERMATH,

IT SEEMS CLEAR TO ALL OF US,

THE SKY IS CRYING BECAUSE THE WORLD IS DYING,

NOTHING IS NORMAL ANYMORE,

SCREAMS AND SILENCE EXITED THE AIR,

NO ONES PLAYING SO SAD UNFAIR,

TIME TO LIFT THE LID,

EXPOSE THE PRISON WALLS,

TELL THE TRUTH NO ONE FALLS,

JUST ME AND YOU NORMALITY RULES, NEVER NEVER,

LEFT ALONE TO CONTEMPLATE,

NOTHING HAPPENS THAT ISN'T FATE,

MOVE OVER, MOVE ON, RUN AWAY,

LIFE IS NO LONGER FUN TODAY,
THE SKY IS CRYING BECAUSE THE WORLD IS
DYING."

Thank you John."

This was to be my last contact with John Lennon, a remarkable man with such a sense of fun. I often think about why he chose to come through to me. Maybe it was because I have a total recall memory and could remember the words he brought through to me. I don't know, but I feel privileged that he chose me on that cold and dark November day.

As you might imagine, being a spiritual medium has many ups and downs. I always know that when something new comes into my life it's there for a purpose. Probably a test to teach me a new lesson. I find I'm always being tested. Over the years I have become aware of my spirit guides trying to teach me patience, not an easy lesson. My friend Victor would tell me that patience was the difference between the mortal and the spiritual. While living the mortal existence we are governed by time; a man made concept. Time was invented by man to place order into the world in which we experience life. What would we do without time? Chaos would rein or would it? From my contact with spirit, I realize that the spirit world runs very smoothly. Souls are content when they have no restrictions or limits. Think of a life with no pressure. Sounds wonderful, doesn't it? Think of a life when your thoughts are manifest into reality. The only limits are your thoughts. That means you have control as long as you can order your thoughts. So my beliefs are that the two worlds are not far apart; only time stands in the way of the mortal being able to live a life that has no limits. My guides are right to teach me patience. I have many limits in my life, mainly of my own making.

Chapter Twelve

Media Adventures

Working the way I do, it's inevitable that I get involved with the media from time to time. Journalists often phone me for comments on national or local events. The psychic press requests articles and radio stations interview me for my views on current topics with psychic or spooky undertones. Halloween is a busy time of year. The eve of all-hallows is a pagan festival to celebrate eternal life. It has been hijacked by many over the course of time but it is a very important date on my calendar because of the media interest it creates in the work I do.

One of my early television appearances came on The Kilroy Show. It was a Halloween special. Many psychics, mediums, white witches and wizards from all over the country were invited to the London studios to discuss people with a statistical view of the merits of mediumship, witchcraft and the role psychics play in day to day life in modern Britain.

The experience was an eye-opener for me. I sat next to a young man covered in tattoos who had a strong dislike for mediums and who wasn't afraid to share his views that mediums were fakes and should be ashamed of taking money for readings. I am always open to listening to the viewpoints of

169

others; it's how we learn. This young man didn't share my tolerance of others. He was one of the most disagreeable people I've ever had the misfortune to meet. However I knew this was another lesson for me to learn. Many are not happy to accept mediums and psychics because of what they represent.

Being on the show was enjoyable. I met people that you don't normally come across. I also found out that I should be careful of involvement with television because they show you in any light they wish. You have to trust them. Programs like The Kilroy Show are based on debate, often heated and extreme. You have little opportunity to have your voice heard. Passionate arguments make for good viewing but it's much like sensational newspapers. It is soon forgotten as they move on to the next subject. This isn't a good format for a medium. It was a good lesson to learn early on. I soon found other opportunities to work on television with a number of differing results.

One of the more bizarre tasks I performed for television was finding toasters in a London graveyard! It was very odd. Their idea was to put me up against a non-believer who would guess the toaster's location. I used my mediumship skills to contact the spirits in the graveyard and locate the toasters through spiritual contact. The person who found the most toasters in the fewer guesses would win. On the face of it the idea was sound. So I competed against a very tall, Gothic gentleman. He was dressed from head to toe in black, covered in piercings, and had jet-black dyed hair. We had an hour. The graveyard was massive, it covers well over three square miles. There was no way could I cover the whole area in the time allowed so I decided on a plan. I would use the first ten minutes to sit quietly and see if I could pick up anything. This wasn't easy with a film crew standing and watching. An image came into my head. It was a large black and gold headstone next to a statue of an angel. I felt that it was on the north side. The black headstone leaned at an angle; the north side was on a slope so it had to be in that section. That was my starting point. I had to find that angel. I hurried off to check with the camera and sound men running after me. The Gothic gentleman was already there but I knew if I looked behind the angel, I would find the first toaster. And there it was; a brand new bright white and chrome popup toaster. One for me. I was on a roll! By the end of the hour I found three toasters. I was very pleased considering how difficult the task was. Imagine my surprise when the Goth turned up five. I was beaten by someone who claimed no psychic ability. The production company had proved their point. Psychic ability was no match for a normal person guessing; or so it seemed. The Goth turned out to be one of a kind. He was a lovely man who was open to discussing his beliefs and listen to mine. The fact that he didn't see life the same as me didn't matter. He owned a Gothic club in the center of London and knew the production company who had used him on various other projects. I was set up for the purpose of discrediting mediums. The whole thing was a ruse. The fact remained that I had found three toasters in an hour with no help. I knew the truth. And I was taught a valuable lesson. When you work with media producers you have to be very careful.

A few weeks later I received a phone call from the producer asking me if I wanted to get involved in a brand new television show for Channel 4. It was to be called *The Friday Night Project*. The idea was for me to contact famous people from the past who had passed over to spirit to learn their views on current events. The idea sounded good so I agreed to help. But this time the idea wasn't going to get off the ground. The people who regulate what is allowed to screen on television didn't like the fact that a medium would be working on a national prime time television show. I come across television regulators from time to time. They view mediumship as entertainment only. Spiritual, psychic, or mediumship programs are limited to the small satellite channels like Living TV. Living TV has made many paranormal programs. I was lucky enough to work on several. *Most Haunted*, is one of the flagship shows on Living TV. The show has a simple concept. A group of paranormal investigators, mediums, and historians travel the country looking for haunted locations. One of the places they visited was Ghosthouse. At the time I was the resident medium so I played my part in the investigation. It took two days of watching and waiting. Television shows are normally boring at the best of times. You sit for hours on end with nothing happening. However is you're making a television program you need action. Unlike some mediums ghosts don't act up just because cameras are present. So for one night and two days we waited for something to happen. Ghosthouse was one of the most active places I had ever been. Replay ghosts, shadow ghosts, phantom animals and I had even recorded voices on tape. But because the *Most Haunted* crew was there it was like all 'paranormal activity' had seized.

When they screened the show, one of the presenters said, "Ghosthouse should have been called house!"

Another experience with *Most Haunted* was at a large stately home in Suffolk. The house had seen better times. At the end of the Twentieth Century it was run down and impossible to look after. It was a symbol of a long lost age of decadence that finally caught up.

With so many rooms and corridors there were many reports of sightings.

On the evening of the filming, I did what I normally do. I walked around to see where the energy was. This saved time later as I could go straight to the places that were active. As usual, if I found a spirit I would work to release it back into the light. I was walking down a long dimly lit passageway with a member of the staff. He worked as guide for people it was easy to get lost. I didn't mind this precaution. As we walked I felt the temperature drop. It went from twenty-five C to thirteen C in a matter of seconds. We both felt the air pressure drop.

Then a gentleman dressed in a top hat, black tailed suit and very bright black shoes walked straight through the lady I was with. Her jaw dropped. I thought Wow! If only we had a camera crew with us. I love it when things like that happen. You can go years between experiences. So when something happens it makes the evening worthwhile. We both knew what we had seen.

The lady told me she had worked in the house for over twenty years and was rather disappointed that she had never seen anything while her colleagues had seen plenty. This was her first experience. A few things happened the rest of the night. Footsteps were heard outside in the courtyard, lights went out and back on. All in all a haunted house.

A funny story that came out of the investigation happened when the owners told the production company that 'room seven' was so haunted it was locked for over fifty years. No one had dared go in since. The story was that a housemaid was the devil manifest in room seven. The shock nearly killed her. Since that day the door was locked. If this story was true it would be like walking into a time capsule. It was far too good an opportunity to miss. So the film crew set up outside the door, handed the key to a medium that opened the door dramatically. He only found an old wooden writing desk, an old chair, and little else apart from a dirty window frame. Much to our amazement, the electric light bulb in the ceiling still worked! Then the medium's attention shifted to the desk drawer. What will we find if we look inside? The drawer was opened slowly. A newspaper from 1992 was inside. It was only a few years old. We rolled about with laughter. The mystery of room seven was solved. It was fiction, a made up story. When the show went on television, room seven was made out to be a spooky mysterious place but the production crew knew the real story

Television isn't the only media I get involved with. I sat in my office one morning thinking, "I wonder what will be next." (Sometimes I go for weeks without interest in anything I do. Then I get two or three phone calls asking for help.) The phone rang. It was a BBC radio producer. They wanted people for a radio debate on abortion. I nearly fell off my chair. I was a medium not a doctor!

But I listened to what the lady had to say. She was interested in bringing the spiritual side against the religious

173

argument. I knew it would be a strong debate as people hold strong views on abortion, and rightly so. The spiritual side of this argument had never been put across on the media. With this in mind and with my guides absent, I decided I would give it a go.

Few people change their minds on this subject. You are not going to change how people think, so I knew I wasn't going to try to convince anyone that I was right. The truth was only the truth as I saw it. What I could do was put across the spiritualist viewpoint in a clear precise manner with respect and dignity.

I feel very sad for women who come to see me with so much guilt because she aborted a baby. Later they were told they would burn in hell by well-meaning members of certain religious groups. This isn't a judgment. It's the sadness I felt for these ladies for the emotional toll it took on them. They needed support and love not fire and fear.

I remember one lady who came to see me. She was very attractive: blond hair, lovely figure, warm, and friendly. She had a small dog by her side on a red lead. I sat her down, made a cup of coffee, got the dog some water, and started the reading. With some people you can sit down, tune in and you are hit by a wave of emotional guilt that has been stored up for years. This was one of those waves. I was almost knocked off my chair. All I could sense was a warm, compassionate woman with deep feelings of guilt.

Then something wonderful happened. Like I always say, little miracles happen every day if you know where to look. Today it was right in front of me. Because there stood a little boy; about nine years old, bright red hair, large bright white front teeth, face covered in freckles, I felt tears roll down my face as I described this young fellow. Now we were crying together. This young man came through to tell his mother he had chosen her because he had known that the life he had to lead this time around was going to be a short one of only a few weeks with his mother. It was agreed on to help both of them learn about emotions on the human side of life. He loved his mother very much and before leaving had promised to visit her as often as she liked. He was only a thought away.

I knew this was an experience the lady was looking for. She was not expecting to find her lost child. She explained that when she was twenty she met a man and fell head over heels for him. He had bright rich dark red hair and a bright smile. When she became pregnant he ran off and was never seen again. She couldn't support her own life let alone a child so she had an abortion without telling a soul. The whole experience lasted seven weeks. But the guilt was with her seven years later even though she was married and in a stable relationship. She couldn't face up to having a child because of the fear inside her. Her partner understood but really wanted a child. It was like she was torn apart from the inside out. The fact that she had never seen or heard anything from the lost child made her think she was a bad person.

The truth was she was one of the most caring people I ever come across. Bringing her son to her changed her life. For a long time she thought she was being punished by a greater force for being a wicked person. Now she had something to believe in and a picture of her lovely son in her head. I knew she could go now and have the child she longed for. We embraced; I stroked her little dog and knew she would be able to move her life forward.

During that reading I was taught that we have to make the choice that is right for us at the time. We can't look back and change things. This also confirmed my belief that when a life ends for whatever reason, there was always a deeper purpose behind it.

So that afternoon I went head-to-head with people of different opinions. I didn't denounce them or tell them they were misguided. I listened with respect, knowing that one day they would see the whole picture. As long as we think about abortion in a human way we will continue to sentence many ladies to a life of hell they feel guilt for making a decision that was right at the time.

175

On a light hearted note, some radio stations ask me to make live on-air predictions of coming events.

I have never claimed to know the future or have an insight into the future. I always enjoy trying to work out the likely outcome of sporting events, I would never predict such things as plane crashes or rail accidents or even earthquakes. I ran a competition on my web site for people to predict future events. I got truly horrible predictions. I think the media causes much negative thinking. You pick up a daily paper and bad news makes the headlines. Good news doesn't sell papers. I hope a daily paper will be launched in the future that only looks at the good side of people. Is it really human nature to remember only the bad? You will never convince me of that. We are bombarded by negative stories; the positive stories are left behind. Next time you pick up a newspaper look for the good news!

Back to the radio predictions. One station that specializes in sport, phoned me on the eve of the FA Cup final. The match is one of the biggest games in the English football season. It was to be contested by two of the most popular teams, Chelsea and Arsenal. Both teams are based in London, so not only was this the cup final; it was also a local derby with pride at stake as well as the FA Cup.

The voice at the other end was loud and confident, "OK mate. What I want from you is the team that's going to win the match, the score and the man of the match." No pressure then!

Right. "The winning team Arsenal. The score 2 - 0. Man of the match; Henry who plays for Arsenal." The predictions fell out of my mouth.

I gave it no thought. I just stated them. Nor did I realize that hundreds of listens wrote down my predictions ready to place bets at their local bookmakers.

"Thanks for those said 'the voice'." Then in his unique manner; "Better get those bets on right now."

I hoped that people didn't place too much money on my predictions. It's bad enough losing money but when someone follows your predictions, the responsibly is a heavy one.

By the time the match started I was glued to my television set. The match was a tactical one with both sides coming close to scoring. The game could have gone either way in the first half. When the referee blew the halftime whistle, the score was still level. Neither side was able to penetrate the others defense.

The second forty-five minutes started the same way. Both sides tested the other without being able to get the first goal that would open up the game. Out of nowhere Arsenal came forward, no danger, when, from thirty yards out, the ball flew into the Chelsea net. No one saw it coming including the Chelsea goalkeeper! That was it. The game came alive, tackles flying in, players cautioned for too much debating with the referee, all the passion that was missing for the first sixty minutes was made up for. Chelsea pushed for an equalizer but left them short on defense. Arsenal broke away and scored a second goal with only minutes left. I jumped so high off my chair punching the air that I shattered the glass light shade into a hundred pieces all over my living room floor! I was busy picking the fragments of glass up and failed to notice that the referee had blown the final whistle.

It didn't sink in until I heard the television commentator announce that Arsenal's number fourteen had been named the Man of the Match: Henry. I couldn't believe it. I got all three predictions right. Arsenal won, the score was 2-0 and Henry was named the Man of the Match! All I could think of was 'there will be some happy punters out there tonight'.

Over the next couple of days, I received over fifty emails saying 'thank you.' I couldn't believe the response or the amount of money people were prepared to lose backing somebody else's predictions. One man told me that I had won him over twenty thousand pounds. All I could say was I was pleased for him.

I believe in getting out when at the top and this was one of those occasions. The cup final was my first and my last time at predicting sporting events. Whether it was just luck, a good guess, or help from spirit I'll never know. But I did know was that there weren't any poor bookmakers. Putting yourself in this position is not a good idea so I turned down future offers.

I love being able to help people so when Living TV wanted me to help them do a program on Psychometry and find a dog that was missing in Buckingham I got involved.

Jane Goldman, a journalist, was working on a series of programs investigating the paranormal. I had come across Jane on several of occasions and knew her mainly through her writing. I always found that she gave a balanced view unlike some journalists who made their living putting people down. They wanted me to find the dog in four hours from a photograph. I'm always up for a challenge so I had to give it a try.

The evening before filming I decided to travel to the location and stay overnight in a hotel so I would be fresh and well rested the next day. I knew I had only one chance to do this.

I was looking for a dog named Misty. She was a gray pedigree poodle who went missing when the owner visited a friend's house just down the road from the owner's home. Her friend had opened her back door for a minute. That was enough for Misty to dart out of the door, down the street and disappear. That was the last time anyone had seen her.

There was no sighting, not even a false alarm in over four months. This was getting harder by the minute. No one told me that Misty was gone for over sixteen weeks. If there was a trail it had long since gone cold. In the past I have found that owners don't turn to psychics until every other option was exhausted. I was going to use psychometry from a photograph of Misty. I would concentrate on the picture and see what images came to my mind. I would go with whatever I felt. I also wanted to meet Misty's owner.

Janet was a middle-aged lady who ran a poodle parlor from her work shed. When I met her she was washing a lovely little black poodle. The poor little thing looked like a drowned rat. Janet had to wash him three times so the camera crew could get shots from different angles. I liked Janet from the first moment. She had a warm feel, a lively personality and was very interested in how I worked.

But above all, I gave her some hope that Misty, who was like her child, might return. The unreasonableness of the situation hit home again. I wanted to help but now it was personal. The need to find her beloved dog was much more important than a television show. I thought back to my guides who had taught me that many have much faith in the work that I had taken on. But it was not always possible to help or reach a happy ending.

Looking at the photograph I picked up a long road that went around a sharp bend. On the left was a pub, on the right an old-fashioned red phone box stood next to a small red post box. I felt the pub was significant, especially the car park and what lay behind. So I would start in the car park and look at what was behind the pub.

I knew Misty was in that car park but I feared that it might have been to pass her to somebody who paid for her. Dogs like Misty were very valuable for breeding. The production company failed to tell me about that also. I believed that Misty was in that car park, was sold to a breeder, and was driven away to start her new life. This would leave Janet not only heart-broken because she loved her but also out of pocket because of the breeding potential.

For the rest of the day I knocked on doors asking people if they had seen or heard anything. Because it was so long since Misty vanished no one could help. It was past the four-hour time limit when I gave in. I felt very strongly that Misty was long gone. But I had one final hope. Because of the publicity the television show would draw, I hoped that someone somewhere would recognize photos of Misty. This was a long shot but it gave Janet hope that something good would come from putting herself in front of the cameras. I wasn't happy at not being able to help but the conditions were near impossible. The fact was we were too late by about sixteen weeks.

I kept in touch with Janet for a while after the show aired but nothing came from it. Whatever happened to Misty will remain a mystery. This story doesn't have a happy ending. However, a few weeks later one of Janet's bitches gave birth to a litter of puppies and she named one after me. So I got my happy ending after all.

Television doesn't always work out the way you want it to. This proved true when I was invited to host a show on Sky TV. The program was called *Your Destiny*. With this in mind I went on The Destiny Channel live over the Sky Network. This is a channel that you come across while flicking through your Sky box when there are two hundred channels and nothing on!

The idea was to bring psychics into the television studio to do live reading for viewers who would text or phone the show. The idea was great for me. I love working in front of a camera, meeting other psychics, talking to the public, helping, teaching and guiding people through issues.

My involvement started when one of the show's presenters called me for a reading. She was a nice person, easy to link with and read for. I told her many things about her life and gave her guidance for the future. I put the phone down and thought nothing more of it until my phone rang again. This time it was owner of the television channel that Your Destiny was on. She wanted me to go to the studio in London, meet the other psychics and appear on the show. I thought about it for a second. This is what I always wanted to do. Having the chance to talk with the other psychics was exciting enough. Being able to share and exchange knowledge while working and getting paid was better!

My first day was a Monday. I had to get up at 4:00 a.m. to make the three and one-half hour journey to London. The show started at 9:30 a.m. and went till 7:00 p.m. so I would get home well past 10:30 p.m. I knew this would be a long day. But when you want to do something badly enough, time isn't important. This was my two-day-a-week routine for the next ten months.

My first day went very well. The lady who had rang me for a reading was the first to greet me. She gave me a huge hug and told me how impressed she was with the reading I gave her. This was kind of her. Any nervousness that I had was gone. When I met one of the other psychics, I knew we would be friends for a long time. I did three, two-hour shows answering questions, reading cards, and explaining how I came to work as a psychic. Not bad for my first day on national television.

I soon settled in to a good routine. The journey was no problem as I enjoyed having the driving time to think. The time spent at the television studio was good. I made a lot of new friends with my fellow psychics and with people working on other shows. Television draws many people together. Working on Destiny TV was one of the best things that happened to me as a psychic. Not only did I make many friends but it also gave me opportunities to reach people I would never have come close to. I found it hard to believe that people would turn the show on at 9:30 a.m. in the morning and watch until we went off air at 7:00 p.m.

I would get home around 10:30 p.m. if the traffic was clear. My full email would take me a few hours the next day to answer. I always made sure that the people who took the time to contact me were acknowledged and helped if I could.

As a medium I often get sad letters asking for help to contact loved ones that passed over to spirit. I would phone them or write back and offer what little comfort I could. As mediums we have a responsibility to our fellow humans to do whatever we can.

Your Destiny was a success. I can honestly say I looked forward to doing my show every day. So when the owner decided to close down the channel, I felt a great sadness. Where would I find another opportunity to work on television as a presenter especially working at something I loved so much? I had learned a lot about working behind the camera. Presenting a television show may look easy but it's all about timing, preparation and staying cool when the producer, misses an out-count. The countdown clock in your ear tells you how long to talk. It also explains why some presenters hold that false smile for a second or two too long. It means they ran out of words and had to wait for the camera to go off. You have to trust your producer. On Your Destiny our producer, Becks, was the best. The show suffered when she left the show a few months before we went off air. It was never the same again. At that point we knew we were living on borrowed time.

I was pleased that I enjoyed every .day. Working on television is a privilege and should be treated as such. I look forward to getting another chance to work behind the camera soon.

Final Thought. What is life for, unless its to make life less difficult for others.

www.dominiczenden.com

Dominic Zenden 29 October 28, 2008

About the Author

Dominic Zenden was born on 15 September 1962 in a small Royal Air Force quarter in Kirkham, Lancaster, England. He is the son of a Royal Air Force Flight Sergeant and Woman Royal Air Force Waitress. His parents had met whilst stationed at the same air force base in 1954.

Dominic is the third-born child, amongst five children. Sadly the first child, a girl named Susan, died at only six months. Dominic grew up with his elder brother by four years, Adrian; his sister, Amanda, two years younger; and the baby of the family Ian who is seven years his junior.

Dominic was never alone. He had his spirit friends. His knowledge of spirit grew. By the time he was sixteen he was ready to work alongside spirit, able to give proof of life after life.

Now in his forties Dominic has established himself as a very popular medium. His direct approach has made him very sought after in many countries throughout the world.

Whether on stage, television, or radio, Dominic has managed to reach out to people.

In this, his first book, Dominic recalls his remarkable life from an early age, with some amazing true-life stories.

Dominic says that the wonderful thing about being a medium is that with every changing day you never know what tomorrow may bring.

www.dominiczenden.com
dominic@dominiczenden.com

Lightning Source UK Ltd.
Milton Keynes UK
22 October 2010

161682UK00001B/8/P